How to Get More Clients: Mar
LNCs" is another masterpiece
never disappoints. Pat covers ii .... very logi-
cal and understandable publication. As an RN who
has spent her career in the clinical environment, I
find marketing daunting, intimidating, and outside
my skill set. Historically, nurses do not market their
expertise. Branding, websites, social media, exhibit-
ing, blogging, newsletters (the list goes on and on) are
all fundamentals of the marketing world, and before
reading Pat's book, I had lack of concrete marketing
direction.

Now, after reading Pat's book, I am considerably
more confident in my abilities to attract new and
potential clients, and grow my business by develop-
ing ongoing and long standing professional business
relationships.

This book is not just for the marketing newbie, sea-
soned LNCs will also find many great tips and tricks
to fine tune and improve on their marketing strate-
gies.

KELLY DAWSON, RN, BSN, LNC, CLCP,
NOBLELIFE CONSULTING, INC.

Craving to digest all the pearls out there for success-
ful marketing as an LNC...look no further! Pat Iyer,
with all her years of expertise in this field, has a suc-
cinct way of capturing today's thinking in a manner
that compels the reader to stay tuned-in till the end
and sharpens your focus on what really matters for
success."

SUZANNE HORKAN, RN, BSN, CLNC
HORKAN AND ASSOCIATES NURSE CONSULTING, LLC

As a new legal nurse consultant, I found this book to be "a must read!" Pat presents sage advice throughout her book to her audience that will serve them well in their endeavor to become an independent business owner. Each chapter provides valuable information in a clear format with step by step instructions to create and market a new LNC practice successfully.

She covers all the bases and provides the reader with the often-lacking advice that we, as new nurses, had to learn the hard way... on our own.

What a wonderful and essential book to continue in her series Creating a Successful LNC Practice to further the entrepreneurial advancement for the legal nurse consultant. I look forward to her next book!

REBECCA M. BLEVINS, RN,
LNC-MEDICAL LEGAL LNC & ASSOCIATES, LLC

This is the 5th book in Pat Iyer's series on "Creating a Successful LNC Practice". It is recommended reading for both seasoned and new LNCs. Pat Iyer offers her guidance and strategies on creating a "know, like and trust" relationship with attorneys. She discusses the importance of marketing through social media, LinkedIn, blogs, and WordPress. Additionally, Pat offers helpful tips on exhibiting and content marketing. This information-packed book shares examples, resources and key points at the end of each chapter. Both new and experienced LNC's will benefit from Pat's vast knowledge and cutting edge approach to legal nurse consulting.

VICKI TATE RN, CLNC, COA,
INTENTION LEGAL NURSE CONSULTING, LLC

Pat Iyer's book offers both established and novice legal nurse consultants a great overview of classic marketing principles along with the most current social media marketing advice. Pat introduces the new LNC to a critical focus on relationship-building for marketing as well as the need to optimize an LNC's online presence.

The author's detailed explanation of employing story-telling techniques to engage potential clients is masterful. We are taught how to meet potential clients, learn what lawyers need, have clients understand how we can help them, get referrals to their colleagues and establish business relationships that can last for years. Pat Iyer sagely advises LNCs to know our target audience so as to market efficiently. No detail is spared in profiling how to get the most bang for your marketing buck by exhibiting and attending legal conferences. From signage to professional dress and giveaway recommendations, you'll find this a wonderful 'how-to guide', for your LNC marketing needs.

SONDRA RUTMAN RN, BA, LNC

How to Get More *Clients*: *Marketing* Secrets for LNCs

Book 5 in the "Creating a Successful LNC Practice" Series

Patricia W. Iyer, MSN RN LNCC

The Pat Iyer Group
Fort Myers, FL

Copyright

How to Get More Clients: Marketing Secrets for LNCs

Disclaimer

This work is sold with the understanding that the Publisher is not engaged in rendering legal, accounting or other professional services. Neither the Publisher nor the Author shall be liable for damages arising herefrom.

Further, readers should be aware that internet websites listed in this work may have changed or disappeared between the time this work was written and when it is read.

This product is for sale. To purchase a copy, and to collect your valuable free reports, go to: www.legalnursebusiness. com.

ISBN-13: 978-1544245096

About the Author

Patricia W. Iyer, MSN RN LNCC

President, The Pat Iyer Group,

Fort Myers, FL

www.legalnursebusiness.com

Pat helps legal nurse consultants get more cases, make more money and avoid expensive mistakes through her coaching program, www.LNCAcademy.com. She is a trusted advisor to LNCs. In 1987, Pat began a 20 year career testifying as an expert witness. She created an independent LNC business, Med League Support Services, Inc, which she sold in 2015. Med League provides legal nurse consulting services to personal injury, malpractice, and product liability attorneys.

Pat is a well-known and respected legal nurse consultant. She served for five years on the Board of Directors of the American Association of Legal Nurse Consultants, including a term as national president. Pat was the chief editor of the *Legal Nurse Consulting: Principles and Practices, Second Edition*, the core curriculum for legal nurse consulting and *Business Principles for Legal Nurse Consultants*. She also worked with her team of coeditors when she was the chief editor of the first version of AALNC's LNC Online Course, which teaches nurses how to get started as legal nurse consultants.

Pat is certified as a legal nurse consultant by the American Association of Legal Nurse Consultants. AALNC awarded her with the Lifetime Achievement/Distinguished Service Award and with the Volunteer of the Year Award.

A prolific author, Pat has written, edited or coauthored over 800 articles, chapters, case studies, webinars, and online courses on a wide variety of nursing topics.

The creator of the first legal nurse consulting podcast show, Pat launched a twice weekly podcast called Legal Nurse Podcasts, available on ITunes and www.legalnursepodcasts. com.

Pat shares her expertise with LNCs through books and online training available on www.LegalNurseBusiness.com. Learn successful business strategies at http://lnc.tips/5Surefire.

In addition, she provides ongoing LNC education through LNCCEU.com, an online learning site.

Pat works with LNCs who want to get more clients, make more money and avoid expensive mistakes. When you are ready to make a financial and emotional commitment to growing your business, check out LNCAcademy.com. Let's work together to make your dreams come true.

Reach Pat at patiyer@legalnursebusiness.com

Client Testimonials

I have been a Legal Nurse for a while, and I have been doing a pretty good job at marketing, but I felt lost because I am a nurse. Since attending Pat's webinars, I have enhanced my confidence and marketing knowledge.

RITA BUETTNER

You send us SUCH good info every week! I always look forward to reading your ezines and other information you email out. Thanks so much for ALL you do for us! You keep me inspired about being an LNC!

MARY WILSON, BSN, RN, PLNC, CRRN, CCM

I have enjoyed every opportunity to learn from Pat Iyer. Her seasoned experience in the field of legal nurse consulting is impressive and humbles me each time I consult with her. She is flexible, responsive, grounded, ethical and sound with her advice. Thank you Pat for each collegial opportunity!

GINA M. D'ANGELO RN BSN MBA NHA CLNC RAC-CT

Thank you for laying the groundwork for people like me.

SONDRA RUTMAN RN BA LNC

A very knowledgeable, clear and succinct presentation. Pat is also very personable and generous in sharing her expertise.

JOY VINCENT

The services you provide are invaluable and you are one to look up to.

REBECCA M. BLEVINS

I am very grateful for all you have taught me. There is no way I would be working inhouse as an LNC if not for you. I really feel good about myself getting dressed professionally and going to work among people who respect what I have to say.

ILENE SCHWARTZ

I sure enjoy reading your articles with all the tips included. I'm always up for learning new Tips and strategies.

CHRISTINA FREEDAN

The CT Chapter of the American Association of Legal Nurse Consultants was fortunate recently to have Pat Iyer agree to present the webinar, "From Cold Calls to Hot Prospects: How to Build Your Client Base" to our chapter membership. Pat is a strong presenter and presents in a comprehensive and clear manner. Pat included information pertinent to legal nurse consultants promoting their practices in CT, which was an unexpected surprise. Feedback for her webinar has been overwhelmingly positive. I highly suggest Pat as an instructor and presenter to both new and experienced legal nurse consultants.

LORRAINE DOONAN, RN, BSN, MS, CPHQ, LNCC, CSA

I was overwhelmed with so much I realized that needed to be done. With Pat's help and the discussions with the other nurses about subcontracting on our LNC Academy Q&A call, I learned so much that will help my business grow. I learned how to improve my case analysis and report writing. And this is only the tip of the iceberg.

DEBBIE WUERL

Pat Iyer has so much expertise to share. I see a sincere desire to help LNCs succeed.

SUSAN KLEVANS

Contents

Acknowledgements

The author appreciates the contributions of these people to the material in this book.

Alice Adams http://www.thelegalnurse.com

Brian Basilico http://www.b2b-im.com

Brian Bearden http://www.upstreammarketing.net

Gayle Carson http://www.spunkyoldbroad.com

Hiett Ives http://www.showdynamics.com

Laura Kamrath http://www.zebramarketingsolutions.com

Gerry Lantz http://www.storiesthatwork.com

Sandy Lawrence http://www.perceptivepublicrelations.com

Debra Lloyd http://www.wp-webworks.com

David Perdew http://www.nextNAMS.com

Tim Peter http://www.timpeter.com

Jennifer Rodriquez http://www.brandwithjena.com

Wayne Schoeneberg Esq http://www.wayneschoeneberg.com

Paul Taubman http://www.DigitalMaestro.com

Abigail Tiefenthaler http://www.sweetspotstrategies.com

Introduction

"What's your biggest challenge as a legal nurse consultant?" When I ask this question, invariably I get answers like, "getting started", "marketing", "getting more clients", "how to convince attorneys I am qualified to review cases", "the sales part of my job", and "explaining why a nurse is better than a paralegal or physician in seeing the whole picture".

After I wrote *Legal Nurse Consultant Marketing* in 2016, I realized that book just scratched the surface of the subject. I find LNCs have a constant need for current tips and tools that make marketing and sales easier. The book you are holding in your hand greatly expands on the tips in *Legal Nurse Consultant Marketing.*

Let's face it. Without marketing and sales, you don't have a business. *Marketing* brings attorneys to you. It makes them aware of your skills and what you can contribute to their practice. You need *sales skills* to close the deal and bring in the case.

I wrote this book to give you more in-depth knowledge of marketing and sales so you can excel in developing your business. I've divided the content into four sections. Section One covers the foundations and principles that create a marketing program. Here I introduce the concepts of defining your brand, using relationship marketing principles to help clients know, like and trust you, and employing a variety of low cost marketing techniques.

Section Two tackles marketing online using websites and social media. You *must* have a website to be found, and it will happily work for you 24/7 - if you use it effectively to show your expertise. Study the chapters in this section to deepen your knowledge about online marketing.

Legal nurse consulting is particularly rich in stories. Section Three defines the power of stories in attracting clients – whether those stories relate to cases you've handled or are the testimonials you collect from clients.

Exhibiting provides a great opportunity to meet your prospects face to face. I built my business with exhibiting. Section Four provides solid tips for what you need to know to have a successful exhibiting experience.

You'll find that certain core concepts run throughout the book:

- knowing your ideal client
- understanding the pain points that motivate the client to seek help from a legal nurse consultants
- demonstrating your expertise through methods of attracting clients to you
- standing out as unique

These are the essentials of marketing and sales.

The tips in this book are based on variety of sources: my extensive study of marketing and sales, advice and guidance offered by the experts I have interviewed for Legal

Nurse Podcasts, and the wisdom I gained from running a highly successful legal nurse consulting business.

The book you are holding is the fifth book in a series I began in 2016, named **Creating a Successful LNC Practice**. This series is designed to give you the essential knowledge you need to grow your business.

Book 1 in the **Creating a Successful LNC Practice Series** is *How to Start a Legal Nurse Consulting Business*. It takes you from the point when you leave your LNC training program and enter the world of becoming a business owner. You will learn how to develop the mindset and attitudes that allow entrepreneurs to thrive. I cover how to set up and manage your business, track your finances, get your first case and create a professional image that attracts clients to you. You will get tips on how to reach out to attorneys and work your network. This book is ideal for both the new and more experienced LNC business owner.

Book 2 is *Legal Nurse Consultant Marketing*. This is a comprehensive compilation of tips, techniques and technology. You will explore how to develop your marketing plan and website, and to share your expertise to attract attorneys to you. Presenting at attorney conferences or law firms involves skills you will learn in this book. You will find out how to harness the power of video by creating videos that highlight your skills.

Unsure about how to close the deal? The chapter on sales walks you through the process of bringing the case in.

You will discover techniques to become more persuasive in your marketing. Take advantage of the two chapters on exhibiting to crack the code on one of the most successful ways to meet attorneys to build a customer base. I wrapped the book up with a chapter that answers common marketing questions. This book has something for LNCs with all levels of experience, from new to more seasoned.

Book 3 is called *How to Analyze Medical Records: A Primer for Legal Nurse Consultants*. Use it to get tips and techniques for organizing paper and electronic medical records, the backbone of our business. You will gain an understanding of how to screen a medical malpractice case for merit and discover clues for detecting tampering with medical records. The book covers the pros and cons of electronic medical records, including how they introduce risk into the documentation of patient care. Two final chapters focus on how to polish your work product to create your strongest professional appearance. You will gain critical insights on how to strengthen your ability to analyze medical records – to gain more clients and earn more money.

Book 4 is *How to be a Successful Expert Witness*. Written for the healthcare expert witness, it is based on my more than 25 years of testifying as an expert witness. In this book, I share tips on how to get cases as an expert, how to polish your CV, and how to master report writing and testifying. Use this book to increase your confidence and skills in what is a challenging aspect of litigation.

You are holding Book 5 in your hands. Here are the additional books in the series.

How to Get More Cases: Sales Secrets for Legal Nurse Consultants is Book 6. Marketing brings the attorney to your door. Sales enables you to bring the case through your door. Your ability to fine tune your sales approach makes the difference between success and failure. You'll discover how your personality affects sales, and how to successfully sell to attorneys. I share secrets of warming up cold prospects and making a dynamite presentation during a sales opportunity. Finally, you will get tips for closing the sale.

How to Grow Your Legal Nurse Consulting Business: Secrets of Success is Book 7. Your mindset matters. The beginning of the book probes how your attitude affects your success, and how you can make it your friend. One of the best ways to demonstrate your expertise is to ace a presentation to attorneys – at a conference or at their law firm. This books gives you new tips about how to master public speaking. You'll learn how to be confident, prepared, and effective as a speaker. I'll also share the 7 deadly mistakes of speaking and what you need to know to avoid making them. The last section of the book gives inspiration - how five experienced legal nurse consultants started and grew their businesses.

How to Manage Your LNC Business and Clients: Top Tips for Success is Book 8. You've gotten started, you've gotten clients, and you want to sustain and increase your success. Business development and client management are intertwined. Both are necessary for a stable business. In this book I tackled how to control your money and your goals, to subdue the evil twins of perfectionism and procrastination, and to get more done through outsourcing. You can reach a stressed out state as a business owner. I share tips for managing your stress and health. Ready to hire an employee? I added a chapter on the process of interviewing and hiring. The second part of the book shares tools and techniques for deepening your relationships with your clients. You will discover how to win over and retain the clients you want and recognize those who are too much trouble. Mastering negotiation, business communication and conflict are essential. I show you how. This is the book to use to build a stable foundation for your business.

Order these books at **http://lnc.tips/Creatingseries**.

Section One:

Marketing Foundations

CHAPTER 1

The Crucial Impact of Branding

Entrepreneurship is not the easy way; it's the brave way.

It's brave because your brand expresses your individuality and uniqueness. Through your brand, you're confidently telling the world, "This is who I am." You're also saying that you stand behind everything that your brand promises.

When you do this, you'll elevate the perceived value of your business and make the money you deserve. You'll find the clients you love.

How do you do this?

What is Your Brand?

Branding is shaped by the perceptions of the audience. That's done through the characteristics we call brand attributes. Branding is also the emotional relatedness that we create, or "brand love." The fundamental idea behind having a brand is that everything a company does, everything it owns, and everything it produces should reflect the *value* of the business. That's the purpose of branding.

Brands allow our audience to instantly comprehend our value. When you have clearly identified a consistent intention and related message, people can tell what you stand for.

Brand experience is the sum of all points of contact. When that's consistent and strong, people know what to expect and who to trust.

Be Clear About Who You Are

What does your brand stand for?

- What are you trying to convey?
- What's your vision for your business?
- What is your brand promise?

If you've visited the web sites of other nurse legal consultants or received promotional material from them, you may have noticed a sameness to their appearance. This happens because so often new and even experienced entrepreneurs don't have clarity on what makes them unique. Without this, the external symbols of their branding—logos, business cards, web sites—have little individual impact.

The Outer Game

People get hooked on the physical aspects of branding. They think branding is about the logo, the fonts, the colors, and all other visual aspects. However, branding isn't about aesthetics. You can definitely choose the wrong color or font on an aesthetic basis, but this isn't the area where you begin to design your brand. The deeper question is what do these things represent? It doesn't matter how attractive the visual symbols of your business are if they don't represent your vision. That lack of cohesiveness will create a disconnection for your potential clients.

The Apple Company is one of the most frequently cited examples of an excellent brand. From the white drawstring bag with the Apple logo to the exquisite packaging, Apple is consistent in its branding. The external branding promises simplicity and ease of use.

Go into an Apple store, and this perception is magnified. Even if you don't need anything, you want to buy because everything in the store is harmoniously designed to invite a purchase.

This is the feeling you want to induce with your branding. When the Apple Company was operating in a garage, its founders had a vision. From the vision of who you are come all the strategic and tactical choices that express that vision.

Your Business DNA

Your business DNA is what makes you unique. This expressed by

- your story,
- your experience,
- your knowledge,
- your expertise, or

- the point of view that you have about legal nurse consulting and really finding your "Brand Voice."

To do this, you need to not compare yourself to others. This is one of the attitudes that takes courage. We all have a tendency to want to blend in and not make waves. Yet the essence of being a successful entrepreneur is standing out.

You need to express your unique opinions about your industry. You need to be confident about how you do things differently. You need to know what feels right for you.

Ask yourself:

- "What do I think?"
- "What do I have to say about it?"
- "How is my personality, my story and my experience different?"
- "What do I bring to the table?"

The Inner Game

Your inner game is what you stand for, your viewpoints, and especially your values.

I'll give you an example of what differentiated my legal nurse consulting business. I had a very strict policy and practice that was rooted in integrity. There are many ways that being in business can test your values, your integrity and your adherence to doing what is right. Attorneys are sometimes the target of people who have lesser integrity.

One of our clients told us about a gastroenterologist who he hired as an expert witness to testify at trial. The client gave him a significant pretrial retainer of $10,000. The case ended up settling before the doctor was needed to testify. The doctor absolutely refused to refund that retainer. The attorney was livid and said, "You've got enough time to reorganize your schedule so that you can make up that time with patient visits." The doctor was adamant. "No I'm not going to give it back."

My client said to him, "I know a lot of attorneys, and if they come and ask me for an expert in gastroenterology, I'm not going to be able to recommend you." The doctor said, "That's okay, I'm not interested." Now the attorney has *really* made a point of telling people about this doctor's behavior in not refunding that money.

Part of the inner game for my company was that retainers were refundable. We returned the unused portion. We didn't hold money that we were not entitled to have. That became part of the brand, and it also was a factor in attorneys recommending my company to other attorneys. They knew they could trust their money would be handled correctly.

I ran the business in a way that was consistent and aligned with my values.

Moving out of the "Commodity" Category

One of the challenges that legal nurse consultants have, particularly those who own their own businesses, is that attorneys may view them as a commodity and do price shopping. Being seen as more than a commodity is essential to a successful legal nurse consulting business.

To do this, you have to be very clear about your value. Know the value of the difference you make and the experience you bring to your work.

If you're new to this business, you may think you can't demonstrate your skills. However, you come to this field with years of expert experience as a nurse. Review your history as a nurse to build your confidence.

You have something else, whether you are new to this field or not: the *passion* to be successful in it. What drove you to choose this kind of business? What makes you special? What is your story? What do you stand for? Who is your client base?

Be a Specialist

There are many attorneys, but they aren't *all* going to be your clients. We're not for everyone. The more you are *not* for everyone, the more value you will have to the ones that you *are* for.

THE CRUCIAL IMPACT OF BRANDING

Also make a decision and set a clear intention around what brand position you really want to have in the marketplace. Do you want to be Volkswagen or Mercedes?

If you're Volkswagen, lawyers will put you in the commodity category. You have a higher perceived value if you position yourself as Mercedes. The more you're presenting yourself at a higher brand position, the more potential clients will experience your value and appreciate your social proof and the other factors that elevate your worth. You need to perceive your value before anyone else ever will.

Once you have your inner brand established, ask yourself these questions:

- "What are your brand messages?"

- "What are your marketing messages?"

Ultimately it's crucial how you show up as your brand. You will be able to also demand higher prices as you get more experience, as you gain more social proof (see Chapter 16, *How Social Proof Gets You Clients*), and you get more requests for your services.

If you are tempted to charge lower prices, remember this: Attorneys looking for quality often think something is wrong with the low-priced LNC. They may ask, "Why is she or he so cheap?" When you are clear about your value, you'll communicate that to potential clients. You will attract those that you're meant to serve.

Is Your Branding Building Trust?

As a legal nurse consultant, you need to constantly evaluate how effective your branding is on all levels. Does your brand build trust in your clients and prospects? Especially in the legal nurse consulting industry you need to build immediate trust by displaying your knowledge and experience.

Ask yourself, "Do you really feel connected to not only your name, which is a big part of branding, but also the look and feel of your brand? Does your **brand** make you proud to hand out your business card? Does it make you stand up and stand out?" If you can't stand in a room and say, "This is who I am and I'm proud of it," it is time to examine your brand.

Is Your Branding Creating Repeat Business?

How does a legal nurse consultant effortlessly earn repeat business? The answer to that question is *brand consistency.* Your clients need to understand your brand. If they have to guess about your brand, they are going to feel insecure. They're not going to trust it; they're going to move on to the next competitor.

Branding consistency is essential if you want repeat business. Attorneys need to know that they can trust you and that they will receive the same quality work over and over and over. If they have a positive experience, they trust you and your brand.

Brand Loyalty

I had a partner once who said, "Attorneys change legal nurse consultants as often as they change their underwear." Really? Do you believe that is true? It does not have to be. Attorneys will be loyal to your brand when they know it, they like it, and they trust it. Building trust results in repeat business.

Consider how this works if you provide a service such as supplying nursing expert witnesses. Your clients expect them to perform at a certain level. Some of the most disturbing messages that I heard involved an expert who was not functioning at the level I expected. Perhaps the expert was not responsive or her report was not prepared well. When you subcontract cases to others, each of your experts is demonstrating to your client base a standard of performance. Each expert affects the ability of every other expert in the business to get work from one of your clients.

Branding is established by the consultants, subcontractors, or employees that you work with. The lawyer has this experience with your brand because these individuals are representing you and your business, and that's what lawyers are going to remember. When you set up your legal nurse consulting business, make sure that your standards are consistent. Clients will come back when your branding builds *trust*. That's going to create repeat business. It's when the attorneys can't trust you anymore that they move on to the next option, like the next pair of underpants.

The Dynamic Nature of Branding

You may be clear about your brand, but in an ever-changing world, nothing stays the same, including your vision. Be prepared to make changes. Your business will grow and expand into new areas. The nature of your clientele may change. Your audience and your clients can provide input that causes your brand to change in some way. You might provide some services and attract clients who would like you to provide additional services. When this happens, you need to revisit your inner game and consider new and additional ways of branding yourself and your business. You'll find a new way of expressing this.

If this makes you nervous, remember that even Apple has changed its logo a couple of times over all these years. Tell yourself that it's graduation time, time to express yourself at a higher level.

In Conclusion

Even if nothing seems to be changing in the outer world, constantly re-visit your values and vision about your business. Make sure that your outer expression of your business matches your inner model. That way, you'll always be a leader in your field.

Key Points

- Everything a company does, everything it owns, and everything it produces should reflect the value of the business.

- Clear brands convey how you are unique, your brand DNA.

- Branding is not just about your colors and fonts; it is also about how you conduct business and demonstrate your skills.

- Attorneys respect, value, and trust legal nurse consultants who practice with integrity.

- You need to perceive your value before anyone else ever will.

- Attorneys who are looking for quality often think something is wrong with the low-priced LNC.

- Every one of your subcontractors affects your brand.

- Branding is dynamic; it changes as your business does.

CHAPTER 2

How to Get More Clients

The number one question I hear from LNCs is: "How do I get more clients? How do I get attorneys to hire me?"

Below I've listed and answered some common excuses I've heard from LNCs.

1. I don't know anyone who knows attorneys

Anyone in your life may know attorneys. You don't know who they know unless you ask. One of my coaching clients at **LNCAcademy.com** had a few minutes before she got called into seeing the dentist. As she talked to the dentist's receptionist, she learned that the receptionist had a relative who was an attorney who handled medical cases. A man waiting in the reception area overheard the conversation. He volunteered that he knew an attorney – she got *two* leads based on one conversation.

At one point in my life I went through training to sell skin care products. The trainer repeatedly said, "Talk to people. Talk to people. And talk to people." You won't find out about your contacts' connections with attorneys unless you speak about what you do.

2. I just moved to a new area and I don't know anyone

Make a list of all the people whom you do know from your previous location. Tell them about your business. Join a networking group and start meeting people in your local area. Go to meetup.com and find people with common interests. Join a church or civic group. Stick around after the event and talk to people. Be friendly. Focus on them; they'll ask you about you and your business. Tell everyone you meet that you are an LNC who works with attorneys who handle medical issues.

3. It feels uncomfortable to be asking for referrals or introductions to an attorney

Sure, it does, and it takes practice and experience, which you won't get if you don't try. In 1987, after I did my first case as an expert witness, I asked my defense client if he would give me the names of 10 attorneys I could contact to introduce myself. I set my sights high, not knowing that 10 was a large number to ask for. To my eternal gratitude, he gave me the names of 10 attorneys, whom I contacted. I got work from all of them – for the next 25 years. Was it worthwhile asking my first client for referrals? You bet.

Once you develop a relationship with a satisfied client, ask them who they might refer you to. There are other lawyers who are handling the same kind of cases. Lawyers are in competition with each other to get the cases, but they're always sharing information and experts.

4. Successful people don't ask for work

This is another myth. Have you ever looked at a newspaper written for attorneys? I recommend you subscribe, primarily to learn about the issues affecting attorneys and to identify the people winning cases. When you flip through an attorney newspaper, you will see prominent attorneys asking for referrals. For example, it is common for medical malpractice firms to solicit cases from attorneys who are not specialized in these cases. If they can do it, so can you.

5. I don't want to ask for a favor

You are not imposing on people; you're giving them an opportunity to help you. Do you enjoy helping someone? In the same way, your contacts will be glad to refer you if they know you, trust you, and believe you can help people they know. If you perform well, your contact will be delighted to keep recommending you to attorneys. Your excellent services make your referral sources look and feel good. Asking for referrals will build your business.

Do the Research

Investigate local resources. Go to the state bar web page for your state. Find out where bar meetings and seminars are being held. You'll also see seminars aimed at attorneys who handle cases with medical issues.

Go to where the meeting is, have some business cards, and introduce yourself to some of the attorneys there. Lawyers love to stand in the hall swapping stories with each other because they often get bored by the seminars.

Put on the Best Attitude

Remember three things when you approach these lawyers. The first is that they may have no idea what a legal nurse consultant does. The second is that lawyers get approached all the time with offers and deals, and they've learned to be suspicious of those who approach them. The third is to have the attitude of "Here's how I can help you." Always put the focus on the other person.

Suppose a lawyer is doing personal injury work. You can be a great service to this attorney by sitting down and reviewing the medical records. You know what you do, but they need to know that. They need to know that your services are going to save them time and money, and that you will do it without going on the payroll. You can do it on a case-by-case basis for them.

Offer a Service

Offer your services as a speaker at some of these bar meetings. Put on a 30-minute presentation that educates attorneys." I recommend you pick a medical topic that shows your expertise rather than making a sales pitch.

Offer to write a blog or article for a state, county, or university bar journal on what a legal nurse consultant does and how it can help the attorney. It will help get your name out. When you write, you are looked upon as an expert.

Cold Calling and Emailing

Although cold calling is necessary, you need to develop a tough hide about it. You will not always get through. Lawyers insulate themselves with gatekeepers. Lawyers have told me that even they have trouble getting through to other lawyers whom they know well. The main point is to not get discouraged and to remember, that for all its challenges, cold calling only costs you time and effort.

Many email marketing programs are available that give you little templates as to how to have an effective email to get somebody's attention. You can research these programs.

A Common Question and Answer

You will often encounter this question: "I have a paralegal, so why do I need a legal nurse consultant?" The paralegal's job is to organize records. Paralegals are invaluable to a trial team, but they lack the basic skills that a legal nurse consultant has. Paralegals aren't trained in medicine. The difference between a paralegal and a legal nurse consultant is about the same as the difference between a doctor and a lawyer. A legal nurse consultant comes in, takes the records, and tells a lawyer what they mean. The smartest lawyer alive can't digest everything in a medical record.

If a doctor specifically writes a report for a lawyer, the lawyer may understand it, but in a serious medical case, one finds a lot of technical language and also details that the inexperienced eye doesn't see. It's no different than taking a lease and giving it to a legal nurse consultant. The legal nurse consultant can read it and say, "This says that Joe was renting from Jane," but that's all they can tell you.

My response to this question ("I have a paralegal, so why do I need a legal nurse consultant?") would be simply, "I think it's wonderful that you're using a paralegal. You understand the benefit of using support staff. Good for you. That frees your time to do the important work. Now that you understand how important it is to use support staff, let me work with your paralegal to make your case better."

Here are some specific areas where paralegals run into trouble.

- They may have skipped over concepts.

- They didn't understand abbreviations.

- They didn't understand the medical terms, or had to spend extensive time looking up information to make sense of what was in that medical record.

Be Patient, and Be a Teacher

Attorneys appreciate this enormously. A good LNC—and you want to be the best—takes the time to educate a lawyer on the records and issues and explains why they're important.

In addition to patience, teaching is essential. A good legal nurse consultant is a good teacher. Just knowing all of that information doesn't do the lawyer any good unless you can teach the lawyer how to use that. You can show the lawyer how this can be used to their benefit, rather than just saying, "This mark here means the following. . ."

"What's important?"

"Why is it important that the mark is there at that time?"

Help the Lawyer with Self-Confidence Issues

As legal nurse consultants, we don't often recognize that our attorney clients are experiencing fear and self-confidence issues. I have a vivid memory of sitting in a cafeteria with a plaintiff trial attorney right before he was going to go into the courtroom. We were eating breakfast, and he had a roll in his hand. He literally ate it in one bite. He was so agitated and there was so much adrenaline flowing. He was staring at me and shaking a little bit. All of a sudden, the roll was just gone.

Here are some stories attorneys have shared with me.

"Years ago a good friend of mine from law school was getting ready to try his first case. I had talked with him beforehand, and he was as nervous as you might imagine.

"I saw his wife the morning of the trial. I said, 'How's Joe doing? How did he do last night?' She said, 'I looked over at him through the course of the night, and he would be lying on his back with his eyes wide open. I would say, 'Honey, are you okay?' He would say, 'Don't bother me. I'm sleeping.' Of course he didn't sleep for the entire night."

"I can remember one time I had a case I had battled for about two years. We went in, picked the jury, and the judge broke for lunch. There was another lawyer who's a friend of mine down there watching the trial. We went to lunch and I said that I don't know that I'm going to be able to shove anything down this little hole that I used to call a throat during this lunch period."

As self-assured as a lawyer looks on the outside, there is turmoil, chaos, fear and anxiety going on inside. Some lawyers say they can't communicate on any subject but their upcoming trials for as long as *three days* prior to the trial.

We need to understand that our lawyers are terribly afraid before they get ready to try that case. They are afraid they made a mistake, and that's where you're going to help them in these medical issues so they are well armed and totally comfortable with them. Knowing that gives them one less thing to worry about.

They are always afraid of that terrible surprise that they have not prepared for. LNCs can help to reduce the risk of a surprise in medical aspects, liability issues, and more. The astute lawyer knows that he or she will be most comfortable going into trial understanding the medical issues are and that he or she can answer all of the questions. That's a godsend.

I testified as an expert witness in a case involving a woman who was an IV drug abuser. While a patient in the hospital she found an unlocked medication cart in the hallway. She injected herself with both the contents of a 30 cc vial of insulin and another of Lasix. Her blood sugar plummeted down to virtually nothing and she ended up with brain damage. The jury would not give her a dime even though it was obvious that the nursing staff were negligent and that the patient was injured.

A few years later I helped an attorney with a case involving a woman who was an IV drug abuser and HIV positive who was run over by a bus. My job was to explain her six months of hospital records. I sat with him in the cafeteria before I went on the stand. I said, "One of the things that you have to think about is how the jury is going to react to giving money to an IV drug abuser. Have you thought through how you can handle that part of the case?"

I told him about my experience with the woman with the syringe. He switched his approach, addressed it with the jury, and made sure that they understood that the money was going to be protected. It would be for her care, but she wasn't going to get a windfall that she could use to inject herself. (She was still actively using heroin at the time of the trial.) The jury awarded $15 million.

In Conclusion

You become invaluable when you share your knowledge and experience with your clients. When you realize this, when you recognize the importance of what you bring to a working relationship with an attorney, you can approach new contacts in any venue with confidence.

Be sure to get my free report on getting more clients at http://lnc.tips/5Surefire

Key Points

- LNCs often offer excuses as to why they can't get clients. Don't rule out any person as a potential source of a referral to an attorney.

- Tell everyone you meet that you are a legal nurse consultant.

- Get over any discomfort you might feel asking for referrals.

- It is a myth that successful people don't ask for work or favors.

- Research where to meet attorneys.

- Recognize that some attorneys may be wary about being approached. Always put the focus on the other person.

- Offer your services to speak at a meeting of attorneys or to write articles or blogs for attorneys.

- Cold calling requires persistence and the ability to handle rejection.

- Be prepared to explain the difference between being an LNC and a paralegal. Many attorneys assume since they have a paralegal they do not need a nurse.

- Be a patient teacher when you work with attorneys.

- Help the attorney feel informed about the medical issues; this will boost his or her confidence. Attorneys are fearful of surprises in the courtroom.

CHAPTER 3

Relationship Marketing: Developing the Know, Like, and Trust

In my years of both marketing my own business and helping others to market theirs, I've noticed several misconceptions regarding both techniques and the general approach to how you can best promote your business.

Focusing on the other person is called *relationship marketing*. When you approach your marketing strategies with the other person in mind, you'll find that both online and offline promotion will become much easier. This chapter will show you how.

Using Social Media for Relationship Marketing

In order to communicate with people, you have to come up with messages on subjects they want to learn about. You can best use social media to establish how you can serve others.

A lot of people are so focused on the tools: Facebook, LinkedIn, Twitter, Pinterest, YouTube, Google+,

Snapchat, Periscope, etc. Think of these as delivery platforms for what you want to communicate. You want to convey the messages your target market wants to hear. Deliver these messages in a way that will inspire them to take action. You do this by having them know, like, and trust you.

Help Them to Know You

Think of getting to know people on social media as being similar to face-to-face meetings. This can happen at a networking event or an industry conference. If you want them to get to know you, you don't walk up to them, hand them a business card, and say, "How can I do business with you?" They don't know how because they don't know you yet, and that approach will definitely reduce their interest. You want to build a relationship over time.

Encourage Them to Like You

The "Like" portion is where you start to find some common things that you can communicate on. It could be that you both love cats or kayaking. It could be that you're both from New Jersey. Shared interests build the "Like" factor.

The people you're communicating with will begin to feel that you care about them. They will appreciate that you're not trying to sell them something. You may find an opportunity to give them a contact that might be a good referral for them.

Foster Trust

You reach the "Trust" point when people have watched what you do and they consider you a resource for themselves or someone they know. That's what relationship marketing is really all about. It's about building that relationship over a long term and giving people a reason to want to either work with you or recommend you. It starts by giving first.

Al Ritter writes in *The 100/0 Principle* about giving 100% of yourself, 100% of the time, expecting nothing in return, and watching what happens. The basic principle is that when you meet somebody, think about how you can help them first. Who do you know who could assist their business or give them a reason to want to get to know you better?

Relationship marketing is building relationships, being a resource, being Google for somebody, being a connector, giving, being a human being, and seeing what happens.

A great example of how this works is in LinkedIn. With LinkedIn, you have the ability to endorse somebody or give them a recommendation. An endorsement is just random. You can be endorsed for things you know nothing about. A recommendation, on the other hand, is a testimonial.

The 100/0 Principle works this way. If you go into LinkedIn and you recommend somebody whom you know first, there's a better than 75% chance that they are going to recommend you back. They are going to recommend you in a way that's heartfelt and sincere, and they will put more energy into it than if you walk up to them and simply say, "Would you recommend me?"

Applying the Principles to Approaching Lawyers

The people whom legal nurse consultants work with are busy attorneys with constant demands on them between preparing for trials, screening cases or working up cases. They receive a lot of cold letters in the mail, cold phone calls, and sometimes cold visits from legal nurse consultants.

They are being bombarded with calls saying, "I can help you get to #1 on Google, I can help you with your SEO," and endless other services. They are bombarded with all kinds of people knowing that (a) they have money and (b) that they are a good possibility for buying services.

Imagine meeting a lawyer face-to-face at a networking meeting. Imagine creating a relationship online on Facebook, LinkedIn, or Twitter. You connect up with them, but you don't sell them anything. You just try to be a resource for them or at least provide them with good information that can help them.

It's not selling. It's more educating, communicating, giving them something of a resource that's going to help them do things faster, better, or cheaper. It's an investment in a relationship.

If you meet them face-to-face, that's ultimately the best way to do it. If you can't meet them face-to-face, maybe they are part of your Chamber of Commerce. Maybe you can say, "I write great articles about how legal nurse consultants can make your job easier" and provide them with some good information.

Educate attorneys, train them, and teach them something new. By doing that, they learn to know, like, and trust you. This is very different from the cold call experience of somebody just saying "Hey, I can do business with you, and we can make money together." It's more about *them*.

How to Broadcast

Imaginary radio stations provide a good illustration of this. People listen to two different radio stations, especially on the Internet and face-to-face. Many like to broadcast on the radio station WIIAM: "What Is Interesting *About Me*." When people are searching out content on the Internet or they are on Facebook, LinkedIn, Twitter or reading blogs, people are listening to WIIFM "What's In It *For Me*." People are much more interested in "How Can You Help Me" as opposed to "Who You Are" and "What You Do." One of the biggest mistakes that people make is to constantly try to sell and promote themselves. If they find a way to give great information that helps the other person, that's where they are going to see the results.

What Makes You and Your Business Special

If you've visited LNCs' websites, you'll see that they basically offer the same services. There's nothing that makes you stand out from the 100 other people who are approaching the attorney with the same list of services—unless you employ the power of relationship marketing. Make that attorney interested in you and eager to find out more. This creates the foundation for the best kind of working relationship.

It takes caring and giving equal benefits to both sides. It's all about thinking, "What's In It for Them?" What can you provide that's different? Ask yourself

- "How can I be a resource?"

- "How can I be that support mechanism?"

- "How can I give them something that everybody else in the marketplace is not doing other than trying to get work, and take their money?"

Specific Applications for Social Media

Don't say, "I'm just going to go on Facebook and be my business on Facebook. I'm not going to worry about being myself. I'll go on LinkedIn and do the same thing. I want to just kind of simply promote myself." That is one of the worst things that you can do for two reasons.

1. People don't want to buy things off Facebook because they go there for fun. They go there for entertainment and engagement.

2. The second problem with that is that you don't own

your connections on Facebook. All you have to do is do one thing that's against Facebook's rules. I've seen this happen with companies that had 4.5 million followers. They did one thing wrong, and Facebook shut them down, and their platform was gone.

Establish an Internet presence over which you have control. Buy your domain name. I suggest that everybody buy their name if it's available. For example, I have patiyer.com.

Pay for your web hosting. Take it under your own control. Even if you have a simple one-page website, it's a home base that you own, you control, and that will grow with you as time goes on. You own your message, and you also have to own your own media.

I recommend *all* LNCs have WordPress websites set up through WordPress.org. This is a popular platform well supported with plug-ins to improve its functionality. After an initial learning period, you will find you can update your own site and not be dependent on a webmaster to make changes for you. This is both convenient and economical.

Use Google Analytics

Start to learn how to read analytics, and put Google Analytics on your website. If you can't do it yourself, get somebody to help you. You want to be involved in Google. If somebody is searching for a legal nurse in your town, you want your site to show up in Google searches. You want analytics on your website so you can see where those searches are coming from and so that you can use that information to help you grow what you're doing.

You can't run a business without having some kind of an accounting system. If you run a business without understanding a balance sheet or profit and loss statement, you're basically a *wantaprepreneur.* You're not an entrepreneur. You have to understand where your income is coming from and where your expense is going so that you can actually make a profit in your business. The same thing is 100% true when it comes to online marketing. You need to understand the metrics of what's happening on your website and on your web properties.

"Is what I'm doing on Facebook driving traffic to my website, my blogs or interviews?"

"Is anything driving more traffic to my site and how do I do more of what's working and less of what's not?"

Content Marketing

Content marketing means you're doing something: writing an article or a blog, recording a podcast, creating graphics, getting interviewed on somebody else's podcast or radio show, or even getting into the local newspaper.

Maybe you could write a blog or something about legal nurse consultants or things that lawyers need to think about. Consider your audience, where they are hanging out, and what kind of information you know that would help them. Those three things combined (having the home-based website, having analytics, and then doing content marketing of some sort) constitute an effective three-part strategy.

Repurpose your content into what is called "Lead Magnets or Opt Ins". Here's an example. Write five blogs. Then combine those into an ebook. Give away that eBook to get people on your list. It could be "The Top 5 Things That Lawyers Need To Think About When Hiring a Legal Nurse Consultant." When lawyers are searching for a legal nurse, and they get to your website and see this free eBook, they might download it and read it. (I have a coaching program around the process of preparing a lead magnet. Find out all about it at this link. http://lnc.tips/CreateOptins

Content Distribution

Share your content through email, through social media and through repurposing. Turn an eBook into a full-blown book or a presentation that you can give at your Chamber of Commerce or a video series. There are a lot of things that you can do when you start to create content to build credibility with the audience you want to reach.

I write two blogs a week and an ezine that goes out every week to the legal nurse consultants who are my market. It does take time, and it requires discipline. I think that's a challenge particularly for extremely busy people who are juggling a job and a business, in essence, having 1-1/2 full-time commitments.

Three Steps to Greater Productivity

There are three activities you should include in your daily schedule: money making, business making and client management. One element is *money-making*. We have to do something to make money in order to have a business. This could include working on cases or supplying expert witnesses, for example.

Another is *business-making activities*. That's what your podcast, your blog, and networking are. It's getting out and doing things that grow your business. You get a case with one lawyer, and complete it. You've got to fill in the next gap. If you're lucky enough to have one lawyer who keeps you busy all the time, that's incredible, but most of us aren't in that luxury zone.

Maybe you have a stable of five attorneys who constantly give you one case a week. Now you've got five cases a week that you can work, but you still have to do things that build your business. That's what business making activities are. Marketing is one of your business making activities.

The Busier You Are, the Harder You Have to Market

What a lot of people fall into is what I call "Sine Wave Marketing." They get super busy, they are way at the top, and then they stop marketing because they don't have time. All of a sudden their case load declines. They say, "Oh my goodness! I have nothing to do." They market again, and it comes back up. It then goes way to the top, and they stop marketing. Can you see the sine wave going up and down, and up and down?

The people who get it are the people who are marketing consistently on a regular basis to their audience so that they don't have that big a sine wave. Maybe it's a little bit of a sine wave with a couple of ups and downs, but at least it's something that's a little bit steadier than feast or famine. That's incredibly important.

Money-making activity comes first. Get paid first. Secondly, always have something in the works that's going to help you market yourself better.

You also need *client maintenance activities.* This includes answering email, checking Facebook, and doing the things that you have to do to maintain those relationships with your clients. If somebody sends you a problem on email that you need to fix, you're going to have to schedule that into your day.

I go into a great deal more depth on how to manage your client relationships in another book in this series. *How to Manage Your LNC Business and Clients: Top Tips for Success* has 6 packed chapters on the secrets of managing your clients. Order it at this link: **http://lnc.tips/Creatingseries**.

Make sure that you're dealing with those client maintenance activities on a regular basis every single day. You can't just say, "I'm just going to make money today. I'm just going to do business marketing today. I'm just going to do customer maintenance today." It leads to that sine wave effect. You have to be consistent and have some kind of system or plan in place to work through that.

To lend some urgency to your adopting that system, remember that your one attorney could have a major disruption in the law firm or drop dead. Partners have been known on the weekend to move out and take cases with them. There could be a change in the law that completely changes your clients' practice.

I understand this risk first hand. My husband built his business around being a manufacturer's rep. He was the go between the manufacturer and the end user. He did that very profitably for several years just by marking up the parts. One day his only customer said, "You know what, we don't need Raj in the middle anymore. We can just go right to the shop. We'll save money." Overnight his income evaporated, and for the next year he was not able to produce any income except for selling our pickup truck. (Fortunately I was working in a hospital as a staff development director, so those paychecks were essential.)

This experience made me highly sensitive to this issue that you can't put all your eggs in one basket because that basket could fall apart on you. Translated into LNC terms, it means never rely on one firm or one attorney for all of your work. Keep marketing!

Making Time for Incorporating New Business Development into Your Day

Finding time for new business development can be a huge struggle. There's always something else that seems to be more important. However, I've found that people who don't carve time for this find themselves with an empty pipeline down the road. I have 3 tips for fitting new business development into your busy schedule.

1. Schedule a block of time on your calendar for new business and consider it as firm as a meeting with a new prospect. You'd NEVER cancel one of those.

2. Don't accept interruptions during business development time. Put your phone on do not disturb, turn off the IM, cell phone, Blackberry, pager and hang a "Do Not Disturb" sign on your office to let others know that you're unavailable, just as if you were out of the office at a meeting.

3. If you're truly swamped, reduce the size of your prospect list. Focus on 10 prospects you're drooling to do business with. If 10 is too many, pick 5. If 5 is too many, rethink your desire to earn more money.

Fill that pipeline now. Knowing how to find the decision makers to fill your pipeline can be challenging. Here are a few strategies for connecting with prospects that will help you jump start this effort.

1. The first is an email introduction. This strategy is often overlooked. Someone you know may have a connection to a decision maker. The email introduction can be as simple as "Joe Smith, meet Sarah Jones. Enjoy." You know what this gives you? Permission! Permission to communicate directly with the decision maker.

2. Change your networking activities. Find out where your prospects network... and go there.

3. Make a list of decision makers. And, call them with a POWERFUL message. Use words that are so compelling your prospect would be foolish not to invite you for a meeting.

Skills Needed for Relationship Marketing

The key to making all these elements work comes down to relationship marketing. I suspect that at least half of the people in the world are introverted. This can make them good listeners and good at asking questions. They're good at making connections. The beauty of online marketing is that you can plan your approaches and your responses. You can more consciously and deliberately manage your relationship marketing. Read *How to Get More Cases; Sales Secrets for LNCs* to determine how personality affects your ability to sell.

Look for all opportunities to be of service. You might meet a plumber whom you know, like, and trust. Maybe a Facebook friend who's in your area needs a plumber. You can recommend the one you know. It won't get you business, but the friend will remember you as helpful and caring.

Be a giver first, and really learn how to listen, communicate and connect. I think from there slowly but surely somebody is going to remember that you do legal nurse consulting and know a lawyer: a brother-in-law, friend, or a neighbor. The connection happens.

Mindset, Confidence, and Systems

You'll need a positive mindset, confidence, and systems to succeed in relationship marketing. If you have these elements working together, you will be successful.

Mindset

Without an effective mindset you're going to struggle. Ninety-five percent of what we do as human beings, the way we're wired, is influenced by the subconscious mind. This means that little voice, that chatterbox that we have running us from the minute our feet hit the floor in the morning to the time we turn our light off at night.

That little chatterbox is influencing the way that we behave, the way we think, the way we feel, what we say, and what we do. It can give us empowering messages about ourselves like, "Hey, you really rocked that last call. You were able to stand for what you know and help settle a complicated case. Your research was valid, and you presented it well." Or it can be, "You know what, that really stunk. I don't think you're really good at this. I think you should choose another career. You're not going to make it in this one."

Although many of us don't realize it, this little messenger can be mastered. We're really the master, not the mind. It's a matter of training and being mindful of what you allow into your mind. We do need to indeed start with mindset.

These realizations are powerful when you use them. Be mindful when you're about to go off the rails, for example, when you hear yourself thinking, "Oh boy, that didn't go so well."

"All right, what are you going to do about it?"

"Are you going to reach out to a mentor and perhaps get some training and have that mentor help you through that situation?" (When you feel this way, schedule a call with me at this link: http://lnc.tips/Consult.)

"Are you going to just wallow in it and go down a slippery slope for the rest of the day about how ineffective you are or how you're not communicating well?"

We have to get our mind right. It was Zig Ziegler who said, "You know you've got to get a checkup from the neck up."

See *How to Grow Your Legal Nurse Consulting Business: Secrets of Success* for more tips on how to manage your mindset. This is Book 7 in the **Creating A Successful Legal Nurse Consulting Practice.** Order it at **http://lnc. tips/Creatingseries.**

Confidence

Your confidence affects how you work with people. Do you feel confidence in your skills and ability to influence other people?

Confidence is something that we all need to exude, and we might come about getting it in different ways. Make a practice of praising yourself for what you have done right. It's again part of the "mindset" piece and it's almost like stair steps because these things build upon each other.

Confidence is something that you get when you repeat actions, such as relationship marketing. You get better and better at them. As a nurse, you've been excellent at your profession. You have been capable, confident in nursing, and now you have launched your own business. Tell yourself this:

> *"Hey, I know what I'm doing when it comes to nursing. My recommendations are sound. My analysis is golden. People pay money for my analysis, so maybe what I need to work on is the business aspect."*

Praise yourself every single evening before you click that light off for what you did well today.

Confidence also can come from reflecting upon a task or something that you had to learn. Do you remember having trouble learning how to ride a two-wheel bike? Maybe you fell off a lot, but you got back on and persisted until you had the skill of staying vertical.

You can apply this approach to anything you remember being challenging to you where you persisted and succeeded. We have to be that for ourselves internally, that internal champion that says, "No matter what, I'm good at this, I'm going to get better at this. If I'm learning, then I'm going to praise myself for what I learned today."

Your self-confidence resonates from within, and it can be developed. We can always reach out to a mentor to help build us up, to help us see what we cannot see within ourselves.

Surround yourself with people who support you and encourage you. At one point in my life I was selling skincare products and went through some really good sales training.

They talked about the term, "The Dream Stealer," the person who will say to you, "You know you can't do this. Why do you think you will be successful as a legal nurse consultant? Just get a job and get a paycheck. Don't put yourself out there."

That individual can literally steal the dreams away from somebody who is shaky in the "confidence" piece of that triangle.

Confidence can have its fragile moment. If an expert witness had a rough time perhaps with a cross-examination or something an LNC did that just fell flat, that's when confidence can be fragile. The most important thing is to reach out to someone who can help build you back up.

When we get good at it, we're good at building ourselves back up. I say to myself "Okay, that didn't go too well." I laugh about it and I say, "Here's what I will do next time. This is how I'm going to do it better." When you're new at something, you may need that extra help. Reach out. Cultivate those relationships. They're very important for your development and they help keep you balanced.

Systems

Systems help us stay organized on the job. Legal nurse consultants often have organized personalities. That makes using a system easier. We were trained to think of body systems, of the nursing process, of how the healthcare system work. We need systems for our follow-up calls, to track sales meetings, and results. We can also benefit from systems for how to approach sales calls and employers and what to say in your sales interactions.

Part of my mission is to provide time-tested systems that I know work. Nurses who coach with me through http://LNCAcademy.com can simply plug into those systems so that they know where they're going with their business. They know what to do. Then they can focus on bringing their individual personalities and wisdom to their business. Systems set you free to do this.

Imagine you were trying to run a business, and you didn't have a system for marketing, or you didn't have a system for follow up or tracking. Think about how much time you would waste every day and then compound that by the week or the year. How much time would you waste in being inefficient? That's not going to work. A solid successful business must have systems. When you have the systems in place, you know where to look for things.

Take the Long View in Marketing

You've examined your mindset, confidence and systems. Recognize that relationship marketing is a long term process. Don't fall prey to the get-rich-quick online SEO, Yelp, and Google AdWords and Facebook ads. People throw money at advertising expecting immediate return, when frankly even that takes a lot of time. There's a science and methodology to it.

(For those who may not know what SEO is, it stands for "Search Engine Optimization." You've probably received many emails that said, "We can make you number one on

Google." This means they *claim* that they can optimize your site to show up at least on the first page of a search for, say, "Legal Nurse Consultant.")

SEO companies charge a lot of money, as much as $1,500 a month with zero return on investments. Not every SEO company is bad, but there are many scammers in that business. You need to invest time in this because it doesn't happen overnight. Keep a long-term perspective. Relationships are the currency of business. Invest in them in a way that's going to give you a return on your investment.

More important, what will help you most in getting a high ranking on a search engine is creating great information and posting it to your website and your blog.

In Conclusion

Ultimately in business if you're going to spend a dollar, you need to make three. If whatever you're doing is not giving you a return on an investment, then *stop doing it.* Relationships will never stop giving you a return on an investment. You just don't know when that stock is going to go up. Be assured, though, that it will.

Key Points

- Relationship marketing means focusing on the other person – looking for opportunities to build a relationship by being helpful.

- Social media is a great way to connect with clients and prospects, people you would never have been able to communicate with in the past.

- It takes patience to get results from relationship marketing.

- Social media allows you to develop relationships with others so they know, like and trust you.

- An educational approach in which you teach attorneys something new fosters relationships.

- Instead of talking about what's interesting about you, share information that will enable attorneys to improve their practice, deepen their understanding – what's in it for them.

- Create a WordPress website that you can control and update yourself.

- Learn to understand Google Analytics so you can use the feedback to improve your site.

- Develop content that you can repurpose for blogs, books, lead magnets, opt in reports.

- Each day, spend time on 3 types of activities: money making, business making and client maintenance.

- Avoid negative people; keep a positive mindset.

- Build and broaden your confidence.

- Recognize that relationship marketing is a long term strategy.

CHAPTER 4

Three Myths about Getting More Business

You want to grow your legal nurse consulting business. You look for answers as to how to get more attorney clients. Beware of these 3 myths. They will trap you and leave you waiting for a silent phone to ring.

Myth #1: I have a great clinical background as a nurse. Just because I understand health care, I will get more business as an LNC.

Many legal nurse consultants have education, experience and expertise. Why aren't they getting work? Marc LeBlanc, past president of the National Speakers Association and a small business coach says, "The entrepreneurial graveyard is filled with business owners who had good products and services." Understanding the healthcare system is just the beginning of being a legal nurse consultant. It is the floor, not the ceiling of success.

Successful legal nurse consultants know their ideal customer; they know what that customer needs; and they know how to speak the customer's language. Through their materials, messages and marketing, they demonstrate how they can use their knowledge of health care to help their clients.

Myth #2: I have a great website. People will find my legal nurse consulting business.

In "Field of Dreams," an Iowa corn farmer who hears voices, interprets them as a command to build a baseball diamond in his fields. He does, and the Chicago White Sox come. Don't forget that is Hollywood. It is an illusion. Don't get trapped in "Field of Dreams" thinking. That farmer could have been schizophrenic!

Legal nurse consulting is a crowded, competitive marketplace. Nurses continue to flock to the field, enticed by the promises they see in marketing material. They come out of a legal nurse consulting program all revved up, ready to be found. They put up a website and wait. Many legal nurse consultants have an erroneous impression. They think that just because they set up their company's website and get it listed in a directory, attorneys will flock to them.

Successful business owners actively promote their services. They look for ways to share their expertise and create nurturing relationships with their clients.

Myth #3: If it is not broken, don't fix it.

You've gotten clients; you have an established routine. You are building a reputation for doing excellent work. Why change anything? In the past, business owners could afford to be cautious. When they found a successful formula, they stayed with it. Client loyalty was a given.

Now it is incredibly easy for your reputation to be affected by social media, by list servs, or by how you behave at a networking event. Attorneys talk to each other–constantly–about who they would recommend as a legal nurse consultant.

Are you continually looking at your business to figure out how to improve it? When an attorney is unhappy with your services, do you make changes or define the experience as part of being in business?

Learn about trends and methods of improving your business. Experiment with new ways of performing your services. Learn from other business owners. Get a legal nurse consultant coach to help you objectively evaluate your business, and look for ways to strengthen it. Take a look at my coaching opportunities at LNCAcademy.com, and request a consult to discuss if we are a good fit. See the brief form at this link: http://lnc.tips/Consult

Watch what your legal nurse consultant competition is doing. If you are not consistently innovating, your LNC competitors will take your clients away. They are waiting in the wings, marketing to the same attorneys you consider to be your clients. You need to stay on top of your game by continually learning and improving your legal nurse consulting business.

What creates marketing challenges for legal nurse consultants?

Consider these common marketing challenges for legal nurse consultants.

These are questions LNCs ask me. Listen to the underlying emotion in this question.

"If you have no experience, is it likely that an attorney will contact you?"

If you ask this question, consider your mindset.

- Are you convinced what you know is of value to an attorney?

- Do you understand how the healthcare system works? Many attorneys don't.

- Do you know how to read a medical record? Many attorneys don't.

- Do you enjoy finding the needle in the haystack, the one piece of information that changes the whole complexion of a case? Many attorneys don't have the time to find these nuggets.

Before you can sell an attorney on your services, you have to be sold on them yourself.

Everyone starts with never having done a case for an attorney. We have all stood at the same starting gate. The attorney who finds your website does not know what kind of experience you have. (Now, if you don't have a website, you are invisible. Having a website is a *bare minimum* requirement.)

One attorney said to me many years ago, "I don't want to hire you if you have never testified." I said, "If no one hires me to be an expert, I won't get that experience." He did not hire me, but someone else took a chance and did. After this attorney gave me the opportunity to be an expert, I testified for 20 years as a liability expert.

Lack of current clinical experience

Do you have to be working clinically to be valuable as an expert? If you have years of experience and good education, will this substitute for not working in your field?

Your years of experience may qualify you to review cases behind the scenes but not having current clinical experience may preclude you from acting as an expert. This is highly dependent on the regulations of the state in which the case is located. Some states require an expert to have current clinical experience, while others require the expert to be working in that field at the time of the incident, or within a specified period. But there is plenty of work for non-testifying legal nurse consultants.

In Conclusion

Are you holding yourself back? I hope my answers to these common marketing challenges for legal nurse consultants helped you.

Key Points

- Just because you have a great clinical background as a nurse, you will not automatically get clients. It is the minimum of what you need to be in business.

- Attorneys will not find you unless you promote your services.

- Continually expand your skills and improve your business.

- Before you can sell an attorney on your services, you have to be sold on them yourself.

- You do not need to be working clinically in order to be a non-testifying LNC.

CHAPTER 5

How to Market on a Small Budget

According to research I've done among LNCs, two-thirds aren't satisfied with their marketing results. I've assembled here a variety of inexpensive and innovative marketing methods. These methods will work if you work them. This chapter contains an overview of methods that encourages you to explore ones that appeal to you.

I know how busy you can get when you're either establishing or maintaining your practice. It's easy to get sidetracked by shiny objects that take you from one place to another. Distractions can prevent you from staying focused on what you're trying to achieve.

For that reason, I'm beginning here with a method that will keep you on track and give you the satisfaction of knowing you'd do what you promised yourself.

Performance Appraisal

Here's how I do it. I use a site called Asana.com. It is a project management site that enables me to create a list of tasks and projects. At the end of every week, I check to see if I've fulfilled the tasks I'd assigned myself for the week.

My tasks might be calling a certain number of people a day, writing an article, or doing some networking. I always check to see whether I really did these things. If I made a list at the beginning of the week (I recommend this), I check off the items.

Even when I do this, things slip away from me, but having an accountability process at the end of the week means that I'm much more on target in completing the necessary tasks.

Goals and Priorities

Goals and priorities are especially important because you have very busy days. To get through the necessary work, you need to prioritize. Here's one way to prioritize tasks. Make your "A" category urgent and important tasks. "B's" are important but not as urgent. Probably you won't get to the "C's." Within each category, rank the tasks again by degrees of urgency and importance.

Here's the danger. You will be tempted to do what's easiest, the things you can check off and give yourself a feeling of accomplishment. Unfortunately, this is a false feeling if you're sliding over the things you really need to do.

You need to rank items based on what is the most urgent and important, what you must do right then. Your marketing is a priority. It's something you need to look at and make sure you do every day. Be sure you include marketing as an A task.

Long-Term Planning

We encounter problems when we're busy because we have a lot of business, and clients are calling us, and we need to take care of their needs. With that kind of busy-ness, we don't think about marketing. We're telling ourselves we don't need any more business. However, when the business dries up, it's too late to start marketing. You need to be marketing all the time.

If you're busy all day with your "A" priorities, maybe there's one day a week that you need to do your marketing; maybe you do it three times a week. It all depends on how busy you are, but the point is you cannot wait until the well is dry to start marketing. You need to do it right away. So you have to ask yourself:

"Where do I want my goal to be?"

"Where do I want to be in 90 days?"

"Where do I want to be in 6 months?"

"Where do I want to be in a year?"

"How do I want my business to look in 5 years?"

People used to plan 10 years out. Long-term planning today is 3 years. You know yourself how much has changed in the last 3 years, so when we think about long-term planning, 3 years is the outer limit. When we discuss mid-term goals we're identifying somewhere between 12 to 18 months. Short-term goals are anywhere from 30 to 90 days.

Those are the time frames you can look at to see exactly how long you should be taking to accomplish your goals.

You can get so jammed up with everything that you're doing that's busy work that you don't get to the things you need to do to really grow your business. Chapter 3 (*Relationship Marketing: Developing the Know, Like and Trust*) has more tips on the three types of activities you should be engaging in every day: money making, business making and client maintenance.

Phone Calls

You may have noticed that email has largely replaced phone calls as a method of communication. Email is essential. It saves time, it puts things in writing, but it's no substitute for a personal phone call.

When someone calls you, always call them back. When you make a phone call, make sure you leave the right kind of information so that people can call you back.

I have an associate who calls everybody back whether she's going to do business with them or not. Like most people in business, she gets a lot of calls from salespeople. Most people say, "I can't be bothered with that," but she calls everybody back on the principle that you never know who may know somebody else. You don't know who could refer you. You don't know who might recommend you just because you had the consideration to call them back and even say no.

Sales people would much rather have you say no and take you off their list then have to call you back 7, 8, 9, or 10 times to see if you're interested in anything that they're doing. And when you're polite to them and when you're nice to them, they will very often refer you.

You'd undoubtedly be happy to get referrals from people you don't know simply because you returned their phone calls.

Set goals for how many marketing calls you are going to make each week. Some experts calculate that if you reach 20 people and get 10 requests for more information, you can get 3 jobs or valuable contacts.

I recommend that you call a minimum of 3 people a day. That makes 15 in a week and 60 in a month. Out of these 60 calls, you should be able to get 5 kinds of referrals or business or interest. If you can't, something is wrong with the people that you're calling. Remember, there's no substitute for that personal touch.

The Importance of Personalization

Showing you are paying attention to your clients means remembering people's name, their interests, their families, their hobbies, and everything else that you can possibly think about, but it's also remembering their particular interest. When you go somewhere, and you're taking notes as you're talking to people, that means what they are saying is important.

I always take down notes when I'm having a conversation with somebody. I can even go to lunch and take down notes because that way the person understands how important they are to me.

I am constantly pulling out articles of interest to my clients and sending them to them. If a client collects images of a particular animal—frogs, owls, cats—and I see something about that animal, or if I'm in a gift store and I see a little cat, I'll pick it up and send it to them. You'll be amazed how those kinds of things have an impact on people.

Note that somebody has a child who's very active in a particular sport, has won an award at school, or has done something very interesting. You mention that to them; they will appreciate that you remember those things. Keep notes you can refer to when you are talking to that person. (A database is great for this purpose.) People will think you have a great memory. What you really have is interest and an awareness of the *value* of your interest.

Some people like to organize this information online. Others prefer to use paper files. Organize names alphabetically by first or last name, whatever you remember better. When you call that person or they call you, have your notes in front of you.

Be Informed

Be informed about your competition, the field of legal nurse consulting and about running a business. Reading about subjects beyond legal nurse consulting activates your creativity. It gives you new ideas for running your business.

Study the Competition

This may sound counter-intuitive, but you should never wish for bad competition. For example, if you hear a LNC give a talk that you realize is terrible, don't be glad. You may think that gives you a shot at proving that you're a better speaker. The truth is the next time the planning committee of whatever organization sponsored the talk thinks about asking an LNC to speak, someone may mention how bad the last one was. They may strike LNCs from their list of potential speakers.

On the other hand, if an LNC gives a great talk, the planning committee members may be eager to ask another one to speak.

The same is true if a LNC does a poor job for a lawyer. He may be seasoned enough to know he can seek out a better one, but he might also decide that LNCs aren't worth the money he would pay them.

I encourage you to make friends with other LNCs. You can get good ideas from each other. Sometimes people hold their cherished secrets to their chest. I recommend, though, if you have started something new and you're doing well at it, don't be afraid to share it. Yes, someone else will use it, but because you're already ahead of the curve, by the time they get ramped up and are doing it, you've already created something new. So don't worry about your competition. Know what they're doing, appreciate them, love them, and work with them.

Look and Act the Part

Standards of dress and behavior are much more casual these days, but it's still important to look and act like a professional. There's so much bad behavior that goes on in business and in industry today. Unfortunately, cell phones allow you to videotape anything; you video people everywhere doing all kinds of things.

You can catch people saying something they shouldn't say or making gestures they shouldn't. You can catch people when they're not prepared, and you need to be aware of this. I'm not suggesting being uptight and stiff, but act like a professional.

If I go to a luncheon, I will be dressed professionally. The same is true if I'm giving a talk. Appropriate dress and behavior is even more important if I'm going to be serving as an expert witness.

Stationery Cards

Send cards. I don't mean business cards. I'm referring to cards that you send to people. When I was running my business, I kept a large supply in my desk. If something wonderful happened with one of my clients, I sent them a congratulations card. If I read about somebody in a paper whom I may not even have known, I might say, "Congratulations on your promotion. It's so nice to see that someone is being successful." I wrote a little note, and sometimes I included a business card, and sometimes I just had my return address with the business name on it.

I thank the guests of my podcasts (Legalnursepodcasts. com) for taking the time to record their interview with me. They receive a handwritten card from me within days after the session.

People love it because nobody sends cards anymore. Everybody sends congratulations through email. People don't get snail mail anymore, so your cards stand out. Whether it's a birthday card, a congratulations card, a card about their kids, you have it ready to go.

You need to have cards on hand because the odds are good that you're not going to the store to get one. Be prepared. I may be going to an event and find out ahead of time that someone there is having a birthday. I have my card, and I write a personal note on it. The person for whom you do this will remember you. I love to buy cards when I go to museums or travel.

Speaking Engagements

Many people are reluctant to get involved in public speaking. However, it's a wonderful way to get in front of the group and talk about what you do.

Some people believe they don't have much to say. You have more to say than you think, surely enough for a 20-minute speech, whether it's a Rotary group, Chamber of Commerce, or attorney group. It's free advertising for your business.

Get in front of a mirror and talk or video yourself. At first, you won't like what you see. I say this from experience.

We do things that we never believe we do. We have gestures we never think we make, but we all can get better. You should try speaking because it's a wonderful way of getting business.

I devote 4 chapters to this topic to show you how to ace any presentation to attorneys. Get your copy of *How to Grow Your Legal Nurse Consulting Business: Secrets of Success* at this link: **http://lnc.tips/Creatingseries**

Business Cards

Your business cards should have more than your name and contact information. They should give information about what you do. I recommend you put your tagline on which emphasizes the benefits of working with you. For example, the tagline of my LNC business was "Experience and Expertise You Can Trust."

Have an explanation or something on the card that is almost like your elevator speech. Put down something that will make people look at your card and say, "This looks interesting, tell me more." That's what you want because they won't keep your card if they don't remember what you do or if what you do is not interesting enough to them.

Radio and Television

Many people love to learn by listening to or watching you. I have a regular program at **legalnursepodcasts.com**. You can go onto radio and television shows as a guest expert. Legal nurse consulting is a very specialized field. People don't have a clue what you do or why you do it. You are a perfect radio or podcast guest. You may be surprised at how listeners can use this information.

People who need people like you are listening to radio and listening to television and going to events. You can both increase your business and help to change people's lives.

Articles and Letters to the Editor

Submit articles to the *Journal of Legal Nurse Consulting*, which is a great way to get notoriety. You can also submit them to newspapers and to places like that. *The Journal of Legal Nurse Consulting* is digital; the editor is interested in submissions from LNCs.

Your articles or letters can be on subjects like "The Seven Top Tips to" or "The 10 Mistakes that . . ." That kind of thing will usually get printed. Articles and letters to the editor are very important. I can't mention it enough because you usually get a resource box at the bottom where you can put your name and give your contact information, or you can also say "For a free report, send a request to—." It costs you nothing.

Walk Your Talk

If you say you have certain kinds of ethics, we expect you to abide by those ethics. If you say that you conduct business a certain way, we expect that to be true. If you say you're going to return a call within 24 hours, we expect it to be returned within 24 hours. If you promise you're going to get back to them by Friday at 5:00 PM, we expect you to get back to them by Friday at 5:00 PM even though you may not have an answer for them.

New/Press Releases

Experts recommend sending out a press release at least once a month, if not every week. A press release is not saying that you were promoted to something; it's really something that has a hook. For example, it might be a new way you're looking at something, or it might be an article that you had published somewhere or that you're writing. Or it could be about a book that you're writing or a speech that you're giving.

Your press release could be about new developments in malpractice, changes in nursing home law, or Medicare developments. It can be any hook that allows you to get your message across. Remember this: If you send out 50 news releases, maybe only 3 are going to get picked up. Good copy sells.

Photos

If you go to a place that's prestigious or impressive or you're with someone who's impressive, get a picture. Today it's so easy because most of us have smart phones with cameras. When you're speaking somewhere and there's a banner, get a picture of yourself on stage in front of the banner. Get a picture of you in front of a poster or a board that identifies you with the location.

Networking

Networking is so important because it means working with people who are influential and are in your industry. **Don't network with people and then go ahead and look past them,** thinking, "Who can I meet next?" or "What can they do for me?"

Always go to networking events with the idea of being of service to the other person. Network with a purpose and you'll network well.

Volunteer

Volunteer for as many organizations as you think are important to you. You'd be surprised how you get known in legal nurse consulting when you volunteer in that particular organization. Become active in the American Association of Legal Nurse Consultants. Volunteer for a committee. Share your knowledge. My 5 years on the Board of Directions for AALNC, including my year as president, taught me a great deal about the field. And how did I get there? I raised my hand, and it was that simple. I just said, "What can I do to help?"

One thing led to another because there are so many people that don't take responsibility. When you do take responsibility, you'd be amazed how you rise to the top. It's fantastic, so I'm going to encourage you to volunteer for as many organizations as you think are applicable. I'm not trying to whittle your time away, but I want to make sure that you do that because it is a way to get known.

There's a lot of networking that goes on in organizations. There are a lot of referrals that go on in organizations. Professional organizations are very important, so don't shy away from them. Join them, support them, and do what you can to raise the bar.

Audio/Video Brochure

Here is a creative idea. Don't send out a boring letter to attorneys. Introduce yourself in an audiofile. It's easy to do on a computer. People get an impression of who you are, and by doing this, you have a great way of including stories or examples of some of the things that you've done. I realize you can't give out confidential information, but you could give 10 examples of different cases you've worked on, say what you did and what the results were. You won't mention anyone's name, and you'll keep the details general, but it can be very effective at getting work.

You can certainly do a video brochure today. That's one of the things that's very much used today or what are called "Video Testimonials" or a brochure of yourself. They are easy to do. You can use almost any recording equipment. You can do it with your smart phone, so that's another way of making yourself also visible and marketable. I cover this topic in a full chapter in *Legal Nurse Consultant Marketing*, available at **http://lnc.tips/LNCMarketing**

Design a Calendar/Hold an Event

Design a calendar that has different events that you will be putting on, such as presentations or events. For example, one time I got together with another legal vendor and sponsored a dinner in a restaurant for clients. From that event, I got several thousands of dollars of work. You can invite a small group of a dozen people. It doesn't have to be 100 people. It can be done for 10 or 12 people.

You can design a calendar that could give you four events a year. You can do one a month. Depending on what it is you want to do or you can hold an event a couple of times a year to get to the people that you're trying to attract who you haven't been able to.

Newsletters

I use different formats for my newsletters. I've created print and electronic newsletters. I recommend finding out what type of law the attorney practices, and then sending them material geared to their interests. For example, I segmented my list into medical malpractice, personal injury, nursing home and nursing malpractice attorneys. I sent out newsletters once a week to different categories of attorneys. I also do occasional print mailings during the year.

I understand that statistics say print newsletters are most desirable because people still want to get something that they hold in their hand. However, trends may change here, and it's important to be up to date on what customers want. You can also take an opportunity to make direct contact with your subscribers to find out what they prefer.

In Conclusion

As I said at the beginning of this chapter, these methods will work if *you* work them. Be accountable. Make a prioritized list of what you'll do at the beginning of each week and review the list at the end of the week. Check off what you've done. This practice will keep your business in motion and in a state of growth.

Key Points

- It is easy to get sidetracked from marketing, but it is so essential to create a list of marketing tasks each week.

- Categorize your tasks into A, B and C activities. Include marketing as an A task.

- Set short and long term goals related to marketing.

- Always return phone calls. Make 3 marketing calls a day; this will result in business.

- Remember your clients' interests; refer to them when you speak to your clients.

- Be informed about your competition, field and business practices.

- Dress and act professionally.

- Send handwritten notes. You will touch and amaze people.

- Develop a speech you can give to a civic group or attorney group.

- Include a tagline on your business cards. Pick one that emphasizes the benefits of working with you.

- Don't overlook the value of appearing on radio, TV or podcasts.

- Submit articles to your professional journal. It is a great way to get visibility.

- Prove you are reliable and ethical.

- Send out press releases.

- Have others take photos of you presenting talks or participating in events.

- Consider networking opportunities as a way to be of service to another person.

- Volunteer in professional associations.

- Create an audio or video brochure.

- Design a calendar or hold a marketing event.

- Distribute a print or electronic newsletter.

SECTION TWO

Marketing Online

CHAPTER 6

Why Do You Need a Website?

Can attorneys find your legal nurse consulting business? If you do not have a website, you will remain invisible to the vast majority of attorneys who might have hired you.

- Why is it crucial that you have a well-designed legal nurse consulting website?

- How do you get one?

- What do you do with it to market your business?

- How do you harness this valuable workhorse to gain clients?

Marketing has gone digital. Think about how much has changed in a few short years. How many times have you gone to the Yellow Pages lately? Isn't it so much easier to Google what you need? More likely than not, you are using your smart phone or iPad to look up information.

Visibility

If you're not on the Internet, if you don't have any kind of web presence, how are your customers and prospects going to find you? Your legal nurse consulting company website is a reflection of you, a digital doormat, the key to your business online. It serves as your online presence that enables attorneys to find you no matter where they are in the country. Your website is a hub of all the information about you and your business.

Uniqueness

You may be thinking, "I have a website." Is your website individualized to you, or do you have the same pages on your site that appear on other LNC sites? Does the website highlight your special skills, or is it a cookie cutter copy of another site? Do you have the ability to change your site, or do you have to go through a webmaster to make changes?

Do you own your site or is it in the control of another person? If you do not control your website and have to rely on a webmaster to make changes, you will spend an *enormous* amount of money paying for changes or will avoid the whole project and allow your website to remain dormant.

Credibility

Your website gives you credibility. It shows that you've invested thought, energy, and money in your company. Websites have some costs to start, host, and maintain, but there doesn't have to be a lot. Your website shows you are committed to your business, and you're not some fly-by-night company. Your website shows your business is established. You may be a sole practitioner, which is the way the majority of legal nurse consultants start their businesses. By having a website with content, you appear to be more than the nurse who works alone at home.

Another thing that you can do to lend credibility to your website and to your business is include your memberships in professional organizations. You might, for example, include the logo of the American Association of Legal Nurse Consultants to announce your membership.

By teaching, by giving information about what you do and how you can assist your attorney clients, you establish credibility and contribute to obtaining new business because you actually are able to show what kind of problems you can solve.

Offer information for free. Give your visitor articles, special reports and checklists. Collect their names and email addresses and stay in touch with them. Those things provide value, and they allow people to say, "Look at what this person was able to do for me. They must have something to offer, so I will go back to see them again when this issue comes up again."

Use your site to attract people. Expert witnesses may want to sign up and be part of your expert witness network, for example, or you may have people sign up for a newsletter which targets attorneys.

Your Personality

A picture is worth a million words and your face makes the picture. Your eyes are drawn to images. Research shows that humans prefer to look at pictures of other people. By having a website and being able to put in a face with the company, your face, you and your role as a legal nurse consultant gain credibility. The attorney gets a chance to look at who he's dealing with.

Your prospect wants to know a little bit about you. By seeing a picture, he knows something about you; a brief bio expands that knowledge.

Your website is like your elevator pitch – what you would say about how you help attorneys if you are caught in an elevator or you meet someone for the first time. The website is like that 30-second speech. The objective is to entice the prospect to go deeper and read more on your site. For example, an attorney more than halfway across the country contacted me. He had been searching for a legal nurse consultant and found my website. He called to say he was meeting with a potential client later that day. He wanted me to give him some ideas of what kinds of questions he should be asking the potential client. We discussed the case.

The next day, after the attorney met with her and had more information, he called again and we had another conversation about the liability issues. Had I not had an effective website, there is little chance we would have interacted. My website connected us.

WordPress websites allow you to easily make changes. Other platforms may be easy to change, once you know coding language or have someone who does who will help you. However, that other person is often one who charges for services, as I said above. Not having to pay for changes is one of the goals of having your own website.

Keyword Research

List the words that you think attorneys would use to search for your site. "Legal nurse consultants" or "legal nurse consulting" are a couple of terms to consider, but these terms will bring back 22 million hits. Instead, think of a more specific term, such as (your state) i.e. Texas legal nurse consultant, or (your city) i.e. Pittsburgh legal nurse consultant. These are called *long tail keywords*, because they consist of 4 or more words. There is less competition for long tail keywords, which gives you a better chance of being found.

Do keyword research on your competitors' sites. There are a couple of ways to do this. Right click on the page and choose view source to see the keywords in the metatags. They will be labeled as "keywords."

In order to define what keywords you want to target, select two or three phrases that are most frequently searched for. Make sure you include the keywords in the sentences on your page. Use the keyword at the top and bottom of the page as part of the text, and several times in the text. Remember, you are writing for humans, so don't overdo it and don't monotonously repeat the keywords.

In Conclusion

Websites are a necessity for LNCs. They are your online brochure. Use keywords in everything you write – a blog on your website, social media, articles, and other writing you direct to attorneys. Please also see Chapter 9, *Attracting Prospects to Your Website.*

Key Points

- If you don't have a website you remain invisible to attorneys who might have hired you.

- Your website is a reflection of you.

- Your site should highlight your uniqueness and be under your control.

- Establish your credibility through providing information about what you can do to assist clients.

- Offer free information on your site.

- Your picture provides the face of your company.

- Include keywords on your site to attract visitors.

CHAPTER 7

The Critical Importance of Website Security

LNC business owners need to be able to focus on running their business. That means you have to have a website that works, that brings in new clients, and past clients back. An effective site has a ranking that's high on Google and on the other search engines. When you have those things, your site will become a profit center as opposed to an overhead.

Security is a key ingredient for your website success.

Why Security is Important

We all hear about hackers. In the worst cases, hacking can make your domain serve nasty links to porn sites and download the kind of junk that makes you think the FBI is going to be busting through your door any second.

In the LNC niche, if you serve that up to lawyers who arrive at your site, the odds are very strong that you can say goodbye to their business. This kind of material says, "I was not prepared, and I got hacked." This is far from a professional message.

Site attacks can happen to everybody, even the smallest sites. They can be very intense, with hundreds of attacks in one day. This burns up your hosting resources. It also makes your site run slowly. The biggest cost to the business owner is that it takes your focus away from your primary task, which is building your business. "An ounce of prevention is worth a pound of cure" may be a cliché, but when it comes to site security, it is the truth.

It Happened to Me

My legal nurse consulting website was hacked seven or eight years ago. I found to my horror one day that male performance drugs were displayed on the homepage of the website. It took a little bit of finagling in order to close the door the hacker used to get onto the site, and it was personally very dismaying. Luckily, none of my clients commented on it, and we found it and shut it down within hours. It made me aware that there are vulnerabilities that need to be closed. You need to have somebody who understands website security in charge of keeping those doors closed.

You Can't Ignore It

It's bothersome when you have the vague idea that you should be doing something about online security and have no clue what to do. It sometimes seems easier to stick your head in the sand and focus on your business instead.

We avoid discussing it. Some folks would rather tell you their most intimate secrets and indiscretions than tell you what their security measures are. Most of the time, they don't really know. They either don't understand them, or they don't have any. It's one of those areas where if you fail to plan, you plan to fail. It's about prevention rather than cure. A little pro-action now will save you a ton of what I call "GNA" (Grief n' Aggravation) later on.

Layers of a Website

When we begin our online presence, our biggest issue is that we don't know what we don't know when we are first starting out. It's a process learning where all the trips and the traps are. One of these pitfalls has to do with how you construct your site.

Avoid free website themes. They're like a cheap box of chocolates; you never know what you're going to get. When someone creates a theme and charges for it, he or she has a level of commitment to coding it well and the willingness to back it up with excellent support that's going to be much higher than someone who's giving it away for free. That's the first thing to understand.

The second thing is to understand that when you invite somebody into your website, you're also inviting them to share information or data if they're signing up on forms or especially if they're buying something on your site. Even when they're just traveling through your site looking at different pages, they leave little data trails behind them.

That's why security is important. You don't *only* want to protect the security of your site and your business so that you don't get hacked. You also don't want the possibility that malware gets onto your site, and anyone who comes to visit it picks it up along the way.

There are some free tools and plugins that you can get that can help LNCs if they're doing this by themselves, but I would almost say you probably wouldn't do surgery on yourself even if you were a surgeon. I would recommend having an expert build your website and set up the security.

Making Your Site Secure

I recommend a free plugin called "Wordfence." Wordfence is available in the WordPress.org repository.

When you first download Wordfence, you look at it and you say, "I don't even know what all of this means" because it is very techie. When Wordfence is properly configured, it will generate the alerts that you need to see and keeps your inbox clear of the ones you don't.

Avoid Complacency

You may think your site will never get attacked because it's small and not important in terms of the website world. You don't have a big site like a commercial company. Here's a story that could change your mind.

This happened to a legal nurse consultant who looked at her website on her cellphone and got a message that said, "You've been visiting too many porn sites." It was actually one of the worst cases the security expert she brought in had ever seen. It left the LNC feeling violated.

If you build your business and you're using your website the way that you should be as a profit center (not an overhead cost or an overhead center), it should be generating leads for you. When somebody comes in and defiles that, you feel an urgency to protect yourself from it happening again.

In that particular case, the hackers had put in something that may have a familiar name to you. In Greek mythology, the Trojan horse was full of Greek warriors who conquered Troy. The modern-day Trojan horse is the little gift left by hackers.

The LNC's site had been built with very basic usernames and very basic passwords. Once the hackers discovered this, they pushed in a Trojan horse that disseminated nasty code throughout her site in multiple places. The end result was a site that was like a sexually transmitted disease: it was going to infect everyone who came in contact with it. The site showed child pornography videos.

On top of that, the hackers hid a backdoor file on her site designed to reinstall the malware after a certain period of time. Even if the security expert had cleaned it up, if she had not found the backdoor file, the site was booby trapped to automatically get re-infected.

If you set aside the emotion out of it being hacked, from a business perspective, this can cost you money. This can cost you your reputation, and you don't have to be a major corporation in order for that to happen. In fact, it's worse when it happens to a small business owner because corporations can survive and come back from that pretty easily.

Having a hacked site can cost a small business owner hundreds and hundreds of dollars because you need someone with special technical expertise to go in and clean your site. You don't want your domain forever blacklisted by the search engines because they think, "Don't go to that domain. It's got an infection."

This is why you need a knowledgeable person handling the security and updating the security programs. You may have a good web designer who knows all about design. Sometimes web coders or web developers know a little bit more about security, but here's one of the questions that you definitely should ask somebody: "What security measures will you be putting into my site?"

That is the question I'd ask web designers before I discuss how much they were going to charge me. If they tell you your hosting service takes care of security, I wouldn't work with those people because that tells me that they don't know what they don't know. Hosting companies have security on their servers that is designed to protect their clients and their equipment as well as possible. They can't protect you from yourself if you choose to stick your head in the sand and say, "I don't need to know about security."

You might get away with that for a year or more. You might get away with it for longer, but you don't want to wait until the day somebody says, "Your site is trashed. Your site has been delivering pornographic email or pornographic images and downloading malware to everyone who hits your site."

Google will slap you for that in a heartbeat. It's really hard, time consuming and expensive to get rid of that. You could totally destroy your domain. If you have built your business based on your business name.com, what do you change it to? Again we come back to an ounce of prevention being worth a pound a cure.

Trends Going Out

Also look at security when you consider certain plugins. RevSlider (full name Revolution Slider), for example, was very popular a couple of years ago. People liked to have sliders at the beginning of their websites because they provided an opportunity to show people lots of different pieces of content or directions of information that they can follow. RevSlider is a WordPress plugin and it was hugely popular, but experts tell me it's had way too many security issues. There are better alternatives with fewer security issues these days on the market.

Another plugin is iThemes Security. It used to be Better WordPress Security by Chris Wiegman, and it was a great plugin. It was bought out by iThemes Security. While they've done a good job with it, but they have put so much into it that it often doesn't play well with others. It will break your site.

You're always playing a balancing game with the security plugins. You want it to be secure, but at the same time you don't want it to fight with your other plugins. That's why it's important to know how to configure them properly.

Based on what I've learned, I recommend Wordfence.

Landing Pages

A *landing page* is a technical term for pages that keep distractions to an absolute minimum. These are very important to the structure of your site. They will help you generate traffic. Often, a visitor has directly linked to your landing page because they've seen something free or special that you're offering. You want them to focus on this and sign up for that offer.

This is sometimes named a "Call to Action." You want your landing page to be strongly focused on having the visitor respond to the call. However, when you're asking someone to make a specific decision or you're trying to focus on one particular action, every relevant page of your site should also have a strong "Call to Action," a reason for the person to be there. That "Call to Action" basically should allow them to learn why they should do business with you.

You want landing pages to keep distractions to a minimum. They're very effective when you use custom opt-in forms because a lot of times you may have seen the same forms everywhere on multiple websites, and visitors just get form blind.

If your "Call to Action" is that you want them to fill in a form to contact you, make sure you're going to grab that person's attention. It's not usually going to be by using a form they've seen on every other website they have visited in the last 10 years.

There are systems and there are templates that you can use to do that quickly, effectively and securely without having to learn how to be a coder. Without going into technical details, the important principle is that there are ways to make updating a website easier using tools. It's not necessary to have detailed knowledge of HTML (hypertext markup language) in order to make changes on a website. That system is getting easier and easier in the sense that there are shortcuts now that did not exist in the past.

Once you have a good, strong, stable, secure foundation for your site, you can add these other things. Some of them are paid tools, but some of these are very affordable. There are systems for automating follow-up and auto responders. Those are becoming ever more efficient and in a lot of cases ever cheaper or free.

In Conclusion

It's important to think about the appearance, functionality and the words of your website. Having done that, be sure that you don't jeopardize your time and energy by having a website whose security can be compromised.

Key Points

- Security is a key ingredient for your website success.

- Site attacks can affect any website. They cost you money and distract you from your business.

- Being proactive about website security will save you a ton of grief and aggravation.

- You don't know what you don't know about website security when you first start a site. Have a knowledgeable person handle the security.

- Landing pages are designed to focus on your call to action. They should have a minimum of distractions.

CHAPTER 8

Wonderful WordPress Websites for LNCs

Why do I call websites wonderful? Because there are wonderful things that happen to your business as a legal nurse consultant when you have a website. In the past, getting training to do this required technical skills and knowledge of HTML and programming. But not today!

You Should be in Charge of Your Website

It is time to have a look at your website and see how you can improve it. You say, "Someone else is in control of my website. I have a webmaster. When I want to make a change, he charges me."

Ask yourself, "Who should own your website and have the ability to make changes?"

Answer: "You."

Do I have your attention? Before Word Press became a popular software for blogging and then for websites, it was common for webmasters to create websites, charge each business owner for a virtually identical design, load it with identical content, and not permit the owner to have control of it. This is STILL happening today.

I know this territory. I started my first website in 1996. I paid my webmaster to set up and maintain four websites. It was great for him; he loved the work. He is also my son so it gave us a reason to engage, plan and fix.

But it became evident that it was not efficient or cost effective to maintain that model. I convinced him to convert the sites from Dreamweaver to Word Press. Now I maintain them and consult with him only when I am stumped.

"Why would I want to add new material to my site", you ask? Search engines love ever changing content and reward sites with higher search engine rankings. One of the hottest trends in marketing is the use of content marketing. This is a broad term that refers to creating content to attract your target market. We talked about this in Chapter 3: *Relationship Marketing: How to Develop Know, Like and Trust Factors.*

What do you add to your site to demonstrate your expertise and attract attorney visitors? Suppose critical care nursing is your area of expertise. How many topics can you write about to show what you know? What do attorneys need to know about your specialty? Here's a right off the top of my head brief list, and I am not a critical care nurse.

- How do self-extubations occur?

- How does the stress of the critical care unit contribute to medical errors?

- What sensations does a patient on a ventilator experience?

- What is ideal staffing in ICU?

- What is a handoff and why is it important?

- Why do critical care nurses turn off alarms?

Ideally, you are adding new content to your site once or twice week. You can't achieve the goal of fresh content on your site every week if you have to pay someone to make minor changes, or load a blog, or new article.

"Oh", you say, "but adding content to a website must be complicated."

Answer: "Actually, no, once you learn a few basics. If you can type and insert a picture of the right size, you can use Word Press."

LNCs can maintain their own websites – using Word Press. In the not so good old days, when I first started working online, it took months to get a website done.

This is what happened.

- The LNC wrote the text for an article.

- The LNC emailed the file to the developer.

- The LNC patiently waited the work to be performed.

- The LNC heard that the work will be done in a day or so (or maybe a week!)

- The work got done.

- The LNC noticed the format was off, there was a typo, or the technical folks did not understand what was wanted (therefore, the job is not REALLY done).

- The LNC started the process all over.

The LNC wrote a check to the webmaster, and then saw another change that needed to be made.

Talk about a hassle! The unfortunate part of all this is that it still CONTINUES TODAY for some people!

Is your LNC website designed so you can make changes, or are you tied to a webmaster for every little change? There is certainly a better way to have the website you want, when you want it, and how you want it. If you want something done, you have to do it yourself!

Yes, you can create the content for a site. After all, who knows better what to go onto a website than YOU! There is no need for a middle man to charge you a lot of money when it won't be right the first time. You can create it (and other sites if you want). Using a tool called WordPress, you can take control of your website. It is a lot easier than you think.

Chapter 7 focuses on website security. It is vital that a knowledgeable person sets up your site so it is safe from hackers. Once your site is created and secured, you can easily maintain it using the features of WordPress.

When you have a WordPress website, you can make the changes in your site even if you don't have experience with websites. You do not need a web developer who is not available when you need help or someone to write code. YOU can make changes whenever you want or need to make a change.

If you currently have a website you cannot change or are thinking of getting a new site, you may be asking yourself, "What type of platform do I need? Why should I use WordPress for my website?" If you have an interest in starting a website and you are unsure of which platform to use to run it, you should do yourself a favor and choose WordPress. There are other platforms that you can use but WordPress should be your choice. And it is for over 25% of all websites are now built with WordPress!

Why should you be using WordPress for your LNC website?

1. WordPress is Easy to Use

Every LNC business needs to have a website today; that is a known fact. An important part of having a website is being able to easily add, change, and delete content on the site. WordPress allows all of these easily and quickly. If you can use a word processor, you can be using WordPress.

2. You'll Enjoy the Flexibility of Themes & Plugins

You can customize your website to look and feel just about any way that you want to by using something called a theme. Themes are like 'skins' that can change the layout, the colors, the design, and fonts while maintaining the existing content on the site.

Plugins are pieces of code (little programs or apps) that you can add to your WordPress site to customize the functionality that it performs.

There are hundreds of thousands of FREE themes and plugins as well as countless of other ones that are premium themes and premium plugins (you have to pay for these).

3. WordPress is Scalable

Your WordPress website can grow with you as you grow. There is little chance that you will create a site big enough that WordPress cannot handle. Scalability means that you can get bigger and bigger and WordPress just handles it.

Some sites that run WordPress include: CNN, the NY Times, Mashable, and TechCrunch.

4. WordPress is NOT Just a Place to Blog

It used to be that WordPress was only a place to create a blog. Since the initial days, you can now create a website that looks like your 'traditional' website without having a blog. The choice is yours!

5. Google Loves WordPress Sites

Google loves sites created with WordPress for a couple of reasons. First, the way WordPress is written, Google can easily search the content which helps the indexing of your web site. Also, every time you add content, the search engines are notified so they can come and index your site.

There is no reason to consider any other platform when you are creating a website. After reading this, it should be perfectly clear to see why WordPress is so popular. It is easy to use, it is customized, and has lots of plug ins. Do yourself a favor, follow all of the thousands of people who sign up every day and learn more about WordPress. You will not regret it.

What does it take to have a successful website? You may be wondering "Am I really capable of handling this?" There are three things that you need.

First, you need expertise.

You have to have something to say that your audience will read. Do you have valuable experience as a legal nurse consultant? Do you possess specialized knowledge? Can you use your knowledge to help people? Do you understand the needs of your website visitors? Can you look at the world through their eyes? I think legal nurse consultants are particularly good at that. We translate medical information for attorneys so that they understand what is in that stack of medical records.

Next, you need writing skills.

You have to be able to put together sentences in an understandable way. This is a strength many LNCs possess. On a website, you are writing for people, not for search engines. Your website pages should be coherent. Some will disagree with me and point out that typos and poor grammar do not matter on the Internet. I think that is an excuse for being sloppy. People who have proofreading skills will spot the errors, which will detract from your message.

Third, you must be willing to learn.

There are two times to learn new skills: now and when it is too late. Technology changes; websites change. Someone is sitting in front of a computer right now designing something to enhance Word Press websites. Some of us feel very inadequate when it comes to technology, and others of us get excited by the chance to try something new.

How much business are you losing by not having a website, or not having one that clearly communicates with your audience? How much money are you spending to have someone else maintain your website? Take control. I consider knowing how to maintain a WordPress website as a crucial skill for independent LNCs.

One thing I must stress - your website should reflect what makes you unique. It should not look like every other LNC website, and should not repeat the same tired content.

Why Not Having a Unique Website Hurts Your Business

Do you have a cookie cutter website? Many LNC websites have identical information on them. The only page that is changed is about the business owner. Plus the color scheme and graphics are different.

Ask yourself, "How does this make *me* stand out? How does this highlight my talents, areas of expertise, skills and personality?"

Answer, "It doesn't."

How Do You Describe Your Legal Nurse Consulting Value?

I see too many legal nurse consulting websites that all say the same thing. "Hire me! These are my services!"

Here is language from an LNC whose site comes up on the fourth page of Google. This is a great placement because it is the first LNC website I found after all of the ones that market legal nurse consulting preparation programs or employment opportunities. But the owner has squandered her real estate. This is what she says:

(My company can)

- Screen cases for merit.
- Define the applicable standards of care.

- Define deviations from and adherences to the applicable standard of care.

- Assess the alleged damages and/or injury.

- Identify factors that caused or contributed to the alleged damages and/or injuries.

- Organize, summarize, translate and interpret medical records.

- Identify tampering in the medical record.

- Identify and recommend potential defendants.

- Conduct literature search and integrate it into the case analysis.

- Identify and review relevant medical records, hospital policies and procedures, other essential documents, and tangible items.

- Identify types of testifying experts needed.

- Locate and interface with expert witnesses.

- Analyze and compare expert witness reports and other work products.

- Prepare interrogatories.

- Assist in exhibit preparation.

- Prepare deposition and trial examination questions.

- Review, analyze and summarize depositions, including past testimony.

- Develop written reports for use as study tools by the attorney.

- Coordinate and attend independent medical examinations.

Be Unique in Legal Nurse Consulting

What makes this LNC unique? What makes her stand out? Is she just a duplicate copy of everyone else? Her website sounds that way. She did no more than list the features of her services. "I can do this. I can do that." Nowhere on her site does she explain how her features *benefit* the attorney. Attorneys want to know that you understand their problems (also called "pain points") and can describe the benefits of working with you.

Think of it this way: The attorney is far more interested in knowing how your legal nurse consulting services will solve *his* problem. The key point here is to think about the needs of your client. Keep that foremost in your thoughts when you are communicating, via your website or a personal letter, to your client.

In Conclusion

If you are not in control of your website, I hope I have encouraged you by showing why you should use WordPress and take back control. I maintain several WordPress websites. If an aging baby boomer can do it, so can you!

Learn more about adding content to websites in the form of blogs by purchasing a copy of *Legal Nurse Consulting Marketing*, a book I wrote specifically for LNCs. Get your copy at **http://lnc.tips/Creating series**

Key Points

- A website serves as an always on duty marketing machine.

- A website enables you to change your sales materials in an instant.

- You should be in control of your website so that you are not dependent on others to make simple changes.

- Although you can create and maintain a WordPress website, I recommend you have a knowledgeable person set up the site security.

- WordPress is easy to use, flexible, scalable, not just a place to blog and is loved by search engines.

- You need expertise, writing skills and willingness to learn to maintain your website.

- Your website should have unique content that highlights your expertise. Stress the benefits of working with you and show you understand the attorney's needs.

- Add new content to your site at least once a week.

CHAPTER 9

Attracting Prospects to Your Website

Digital marketing is not about numbers, except for one: your website's ranking on a search engine. How readily a potential customer or client finds your site is important for legal nurse consultants who are either independent or who work in law firms and other agencies. You need to know how search engines work and how to write content that will make it easy for those who need your services to find you.

Learn the Principles and Skip the Fads

The specific *tactics* search engines use frequently change. The tactics may change, but the *principles* remain constant. Tactical methods change, but the important principle is to create a website that gets traffic.

Remember that advertising has been around for a long time. A book called *Scientific Advertising* published by Claude C. Hopkins in 1923 proposes that advertising consists of gaining awareness of your product, attracting the interest of those who look more closely, turning that interest into desire, and then turning that desire into action. We've simply switched the medium to the Internet.

We use principles to make sure people find our websites. If you cannot be found by search engines, if you cannot be found in social media, for all intents and purposes today, you don't exist. One of the principles is to provide content on your website that focuses on your attorney client's needs. Listen to the client. Use the data to drive your decisions, test to see what's working, and let the market tell you what's actually working. Once you learn those kinds of things, it becomes much simpler to adapt as new tactics, new techniques, and new tools come into play.

Search Methods

Once upon a time there used to be something that people had in their houses called a phone book. Mine is holding up my monitor right now, and most phone books are used for this purpose or as paperweights.

Now people search on their mobile phones or computers. Seventy-five to eighty-five percent of the population in this country is never more than three feet away from their mobile phones at any time.

It is critical that you can be found. You want your website to appear so that you can help them answer their questions.

How You Get Found

"Search Engine Optimization," also abbreviated as "SEO," is a term you're sure to hear in connection with how your site is found. Why should you care about it?

Search Engine Optimization is the set of techniques and tactics that we use to ensure that when somebody searches for you, your website comes up. Your website appears in the search results and, ideally, you're the top of the search results.

There's a joke that if you want to hide something from people, the best place to hide it is on Page 2 of Google. If you're not on the top of the page, people simply don't click through. Google is trying to give customers the best answer. Google gets most of the search traffic, so it tends to be the search engine we focus on.

Search engine optimization is about making sure that your website appears or that your content appears when people ask relevant questions. Your content should address the questions attorneys commonly have. It may have more meaning for you if you think of it as ACQ: "Answering Customer Questions."

It's very easy to get overwhelmed by all the various techniques and dark magic that people talk about in terms of how you appear at the top of Google. Instead, focus on this: Are you answering customer questions effectively? Are you helping your customers to get where they need to in their customer journey and to help them at their exact point of need?

Content is All-important

It helps to understand how Google works. It employs technology that reads your website. It actually looks at the content; it is relatively sophisticated. Search engines use what's called an *algorithm* or spider. This is basically a bit of technology that can look at your content and to a degree understand what this content is about.

When a potential client goes to Google right now and types in a specific thing, they're asking a question. They're saying, "I'm looking for a legal nurse consultant" or "I'm looking for a legal consultant" because maybe they haven't thought about the nurse part or they're thinking about a malpractice suit.

They're asking a question. Google looks at your content to determine: "Does this page address the topic? Is this page relevant to what the person asking this question is trying to find out?"

The second important factor which affects your website is: "Do people link to this content?" Obviously, if other people are linking to your content, that's a vote this is a good answer to a question somebody might have.

The combined quality of the content and of the links helps reveal your site has pages that answer the question the customers had when they typed in their keywords.

Don't Try to Game the System

Your content's relevance is an important issue. You may remember when websites created by unscrupulous people were stuffed with keywords, particularly of a pornographic nature, in an attempt to get a person to a website. Google caught on to that particular strategy and decided that it was going to stamp it out.

Be aware that Google is very, very smart. If someone approaches you with an offer to outsmart Google, say no. A business strategy that tries to be smarter than Google probably won't work. They have a lot of really smart folks who spend all day trying to make sure that people don't game the system.

People who try to game the system are the bad guys in Google's world. They have a full team called the "Google Web-Spam Team." This team spends a lot of their day tweaking the algorithm and tuning the machine to ensure that pages with bad answers to questions never appear. Google will blacklist sites and knock them out of the search results either for indefinite periods or in some cases permanently, based on people trying to scam the system. Don't be that person.

How to Use Keywords

You'll use keywords on your website to attract attorneys. Let's say you offer services to medical malpractice attorneys. You might decide to use "medical malpractice" as a keyword. Google has had trouble with people who use a word too often. What is the correct frequency? Following are some guidelines for correct usage .You might hear or read that it should never be more than 5%, or it should never be less than 1% and etc. That's probably thinking about it too mechanistically.

Instead, focus on the distinctness of your term. Let's take medical malpractice as an example. If you have a short bit of content on the page, the percentage of time a word like medical malpractice might appear is going to be relatively high. You might have to use it four, five, or six times on the page. If your page has a hundred-word definition of medical malpractice, it's hard not to have it frequently appear. What's important is that it appears *organically* or how it would sound if you were simply talking to a person about it. If you're writing a lengthy page, 1,000 words or 1,500 words, it's entirely possible that your keyword frequency is going to be lower because you're going to get into more nuances and detail. You might use more synonyms for medical malpractice. Think about the best way to answer questions your customers have.

You know the questions that customers ask you constantly. You know how to answer them. Create your content about the questions.

The term "medical malpractice" will appears relatively naturally, and its frequency will probably fall somewhere between that 1% and 5%. You don't need to play with it too much. Realistically, you do want to target 300 or 400 words as a minimum on a page. If you have 300 to 400 words and the phrase has only appeared once, use it a couple of more times just to make sure it's clearer to Google that's what you're writing about.

This isn't *keyword stuffing* (excess use of a keyword) but simply making it very clear that this is the topic of the page. If you have a lengthy page, your keyword frequency might be a little lower and that's okay. Don't get hung up on the frequency instead of ensuring that the term appears in a natural way.

Bad and Good Examples of Use of Keywords

This is a bad use of keywords. Keyword stuffing would read like,

> "Are you an attorney handling a medical malpractice case? I'm a legal nurse consultant who can help with medical malpractice cases so that you take valid medical malpractice cases and you don't end up losing your medical malpractice cases and spending a lot of time unnecessarily on your medical malpractice cases."

This type of writing raises red flags for Google. They look at it and say, "Okay, that's not the way people talk."

This is more natural:

> "Are you an attorney focused on medical malpractice cases or are you a legal nurse consultant helping attorneys with those kinds of cases?"

Repeated use of "medical malpractice" will look unnatural. Instead, use related terms. You might include medical malpractice, malpractice, malpractice case, and professional negligence. It will be clear to Google what the page is about. It comes down to this: *Write for people. Don't write for the search engines.*

Checking Your Effectiveness

You can use a number of tools to check the effectiveness of your writing. If you're using something like WordPress, the

Yoast SEO plugin is one that I particularly like. It will give you quick feedback on the effectiveness of your use of keywords, and suggest ways to improve. You'll get a red (bad), yellow (could be improved) or green (great job) grade.

The Yoast SEO plugin tells you you've checked the right boxes to ensure that your content is easily read, has the keyword present, and isn't reusing a keyword that you've used again and again." When that happens, you will have pages on your own site that will compete with one another for Google's attention. Yoast helps you get a really good sense of whether or not your content is structured correctly to help Google understand what you're talking about.

When Writing Content, Think Like a Reporter

Reporters are always taught to answer a series of questions: "Who, what, where, when, why and how?" Apply these principles to answer questions for your clients.

"Who are you talking about?"

"What are you talking about?"

"Where does it matter?"

"When does it matter?"

"Why does it matter?"

"How can they learn more or take the next step?"

Be logical and clear to help attorneys get their questions answered.

Be Focused

Sharp content is focused on a clear point. What is the point of the page? Be clear about that throughout. For instance, if an LNC is writing a piece or a page about medical malpractice, what's the point of the page?

- Is it to answer a potential client's question about how the LNC helps attorneys?

- Is it to explain how an LNC helps attorneys in ways different than a paralegal does?

- Is it to give an example of a case the LNC worked on?

- Is it to recruit healthcare providers who want to review cases for the LNC firm?

- Is it why you should choose this LNC to help the attorney with the case?

Spell out these choices. One of the problems a lot of websites have is that their pages try to do too much work, and customers get lost as they're reading them because they can't actually figure out (a) what their point is and (b) what the appropriate next step is.

Digestible Content

Make your content easily digestible, which can mean that the content on the page is short. Since you want to target at least 300 to 400 words, it also means chunking up that content with devices like headlines and bullet points so that attorneys can look at it quickly to get their question answered and then take the appropriate next step.

Shareable Content

Social media plays a huge role in how your content becomes available because maybe the person who finds you isn't the attorney who is handling a case with medical issues. Maybe it's that person's colleague. Maybe it's that person's spouse. Maybe it's a friend of theirs who says, "I know you were concerned about getting help with your case. Here is a site you should check out."

Give your visitors a reason and a way to share. Follow these tips:

- Make your content emotionally compelling. Tell a story; use vivid language.

- Add a share button that enables the visitor to email content to a colleague.

- Make sure that the page's headline is a length that fits in a tweet. It needs to be 140 characters or less so it can be shared without going over the limits.

Using Others' Content

Legal nurse consultants ask me, "Is it okay if I copy a news article and place it on my website?" For example, the article is about a large personal injury verdict, and you want to put the entire article on your website. The questions that come up are,

- "How much can I share?

- "When is it too much?"

- "How much of other people's content should I be sharing?"

Think in terms of the way you cite content when you are writing papers in school. It's okay to take a couple of sentences, a very short paragraph, or maybe even a quote that illustrates the point the original author was making. Then include a link and a citation.

You can write for instance, "As I was reading the other day on so-and-so's blog or on so-and-so's website. . ." The website reference would be a link to that website. Follow with the quote. Use the block quote tag if you're actually pulling content. If you're not familiar with HTML, have your web developer give you a tool to create a block quote tag to put content in quotes. Make sure there's a link back to the original content so people can find it.

Google rewards links to other sites. Not everyone is an expert in everything. Some people are very good writers, and they have said it better than you're going to. Sometimes there's no need to be redundant even if they didn't say it brilliantly. Save yourself some time and say, "I saw this on so-and-so's website. You should check that out. Here's why it supports my point," and then continue with your point.

To summarize, we can certainly include content that other people have written as long as it's well attributed, it's brief or a short quote, and it's relevant to the information that you're covering on your page.

Don't plagiarize anyone. Be clear who the original author of that information was. Your citations illustrate to your potential clients that you are a resource. You are well connected to other thought leaders in your industry.

Sharing content will help you show up in social media and/or searches because it shows that you're more relevant. It will help the other folks whose content you are quoting, which generally positions them well and can help you build relationships within your industry. It's ethically the right way to handle it. You're being very conscious of not plagiarizing somebody else's material but instead using it and building on it to support your point and help your customers address their needs.

When Someone Uses Your Content

I once wrote a summary of a Texas case that resulted in a huge verdict of $312 million involving a nursing home resident who developed pressure sores. I was surprised when I found my exact summary in my words *without* attribution on another LNC's website. The LNC implied that she was the individual who helped the attorney obtain that verdict. I don't believe that was true.

There's nothing wrong with sending that person an email saying, "I'm glad you found so much value out of my content. I would really appreciate if you would link to me."

If they ignore you, you can send them another follow-up that says, "I've tried to reach out to you a couple of times. If you're not able to put a link, I would really appreciate it if you take that down."

Using others' content without attribution is unfair. It happens frequently enough that it's something to be conscious about. You certainly don't want to be the person doing that to somebody else. Just build on what people are doing, certainly give them credit and you will find yourself enmeshed in a community of others who act the same way. They will tend to be great people.

Citations Enlarge Your Networking Circle

I've met some wonderful people because I cited something they said in a blog post that I wrote or in content that I wrote for my site. It has also led to profitable business relationships where we've been able to funnel leads to one another and help each other grow our practices.

A colleague says that 30% of his business in the past year came because of introductions made by a single person who he first linked to on his blog nine years ago. Twenty percent more came from another small group of people to whom he's linked to over the years as well.

It really does pay off in the long run. That didn't happen overnight. It didn't happen instantly by any stretch, but you build a relationship. You show yourself as an ethical and credible person who's willing to assist others, and help them grow. You will reap the rewards many times over.

In Conclusion

If you apply the principles in this chapter, you will have the tools you need to make your web site a magnet for the clients you want to attract. Please see Chapter 6, *Why Do You Need a Website?* for more information about how to enhance your website.

Key Points

- Digital marketing is not about numbers, except for one: your website's ranking on a search engine.

- Learn the principles and skip the fads.

- If you cannot be found by search engines, if you cannot be found in social media, for all intents and purposes today, you don't exist.

- Seventy-five to eighty-five percent of the population in this country is never more than three feet away from their mobile phones at any time. Your site has to be findable through mobile searches.

- Focus your website content on answering customer questions effectively. Google evaluates how well you answer search questions.

- Don't try to game the system. Provide relevant content.

- Use keywords on your page in content that sounds like you are simply talking to a person. Write for people, don't write for the search engines.

- Anticipate and answer the prospect's questions by thinking like a reporter: who, where, why, how, and when.

- Write focused, digestible and shareable content.

- Cite the source of content you use that someone else wrote. If you see your content being shared without citation, contact that person to request attribution.

CHAPTER 10

Secrets of Driving Traffic to Your Website

Around the late 1990s or early 2000s the real big buzzword was *ecommerce*. People realized they could make money on the Internet by selling things through ecommerce. That's when the whole big Internet marketing push began.

Today it makes sense for a legal nurse consultant to view her/his website as both a marketing tool and potentially an arena for direct sales. First, though, you need to get traffic. This is of particular concern to small business owners.

If you are most legal nurse consultants, you want to share your knowledge with prospects and attorney clients. You want your website to attract clients to show what you can do to help the attorney.

Avoid Fallacies

Too many people are entranced by the statement from the movie, *Field of Dreams*: "If you build it, they will come." People think they will have a website built, have their online real estate, and visitors will come to their door.

That's not true. You can have a website, but if nobody knows about it, they're not going to find you. They're not going to come to your door. That's why traffic is so important. When you build your website, that's only Step 1 of many different things that have to happen in order to be successful online.

To use an analogy, I write and publish many books. I know that you don't write the book and publish it, and that's the end of what you need to do. You have to promote it. You have to get the word out. In some cases, people do book tours. There's a whole plan in place in order to become a successful author. The same thing is true with your website.

Tell people about your site. Send an email to your friends and family saying, "Hey, go check out my website." That's a form of traffic. People are going to your website. Ask them what they think of it. Is it attractive? Easy to navigate?

Social Media

Once people give you their opinions, you need to engage with social media. A lot of times people pooh-pooh social media, thinking it's just a fad or nobody is really doing things with it. Social media is essential to drive traffic to your website.

With social media (specifically, Facebook, LinkedIn and Twitter), you can easily tell people about your website, what you're doing, and provide a link back to your website or back to that blog post or article.

If you're on Facebook, you automatically have an audience of people who are your friends, contacts, or business associates. The same is true with LinkedIn. When you publish something on your wall or you post an article, you can have a link back to your website, and people will find you that way.

These are cost-free methods. You can send out a tweet on Twitter to people and let them know about a great article. Include an image so it will catch their attention. That in itself will get people to your website.

There are other ways where you can pay for advertising. You can do things with Facebook Ads or Google Ads. You have probably seen these on the side when you log into Facebook. These ads can help you get targeted to the audience you want to reach.

When you just post on your Facebook wall, who's going to see it except your friends, family and acquaintances? If legal nurse consulting is your niche and you want to attract and work with attorneys, chances are the people that you interact with on Facebook aren't all attorneys. You may think, "If I post it on my wall, all my friends and family are going to see it, but that's not going to get me business."

When you actually pay for that traffic or ads, you can say, "I want to show this ad to attorneys in this particular geographic area with this type of specialty." You can narrow down the demographics of who is going to see your ad. When they see that, they're going to click on it, and that can drive traffic to your website.

Target Your Market

Put some thought into your target market that you want to attract. Do you need the skills? You are going to start probably with no skills in the beginning and learn along the way, or you can hire an LNC business coach to help you with that. (See LNCAcademy.com for details of Pat Iyer's coaching program.)

One important consideration is your time frame. A lot of times people say, "I just wanted to use free traffic." Free traffic is absolutely beautiful. Nobody will say that they don't want free traffic. You will get organic results in Google, meaning when you put your website up, Google finds and indexes it. When somebody types in "Legal Nurse Consultants in New York," it's not a sure thing that your website will automatically be found and ranked highly in Google. If you don't do anything, if you don't pay, and you're just looking for free traffic, it will happen, but it's going to take a long time.

If you go with paid traffic, that's almost instant results because you're paying to get that traffic to your website. You *can* learn how to do advertising well. You can set aside a small budget. I do mean small. You can start marketing things for as little as $5 a day on Facebook. I recommend you find a knowledgeable person to help you build a Facebook ad campaign. The system Facebook uses changes often; there are nuances to using it that experts understand.

Should You be Advertising?

This book focuses on marketing and sales and is based on the assumption you want more business. If you do, think about who your target audience is going to be and what your timeframe is. If you're a legal nurse consultant now who is also working a full time job, maybe doing all that advertising would *not* be advantageous.

One of the big setbacks we can have as a small business is that spurt of growth that we're not ready for. You may be working full time and doing LNC work on the side. If you get a heavy case load from many attorneys at once, that's not going to be manageable for you. You will find that influx to be stressful situation and will necessitate having time management and delegation skills. . However, if you are in business full-time or three-quarters time and you need a steady stream of business, certainly paid traffic is going to significantly help you.

At one point in my legal nurse consulting business when we were working on volumes of cases. They were all related to people who were suing because of defective medical devices. The law firm sent a truck with medical records. The driver offloaded 24 copy paper case size boxes with medical records in them. It was like an elephant that took over every bit of space in our office. It swamped everything else in our practice.

Consider this a cautionary tale. If you are pushing hard to get business in, you have to be prepared for handling the business. It's not enough to get the cases in the door. Your business success is shaped by what you do with them, how you distribute them, how you work with subcontractors if that's your model, and then how that fits in to the other parts of your life.

This also points out how building up your website is part of this flow. If you want your website to be found through advertising and social media, you also have to be prepared for more work. Look at the big picture of everything that you're doing and managing it all together.

The dilemma for independent legal nurse consultants is that they really don't have much control over the thought processes of their clients. The clients suddenly decide that they're going to clear their desks, send work out to their legal nurse consultants, and the cases may all come in at one time.

Other Traffic Myths

You don't just want *anybody* coming to your website. People think, "If I can just get eyeballs on my website or if I can just get people there, it will happen." Here's an analogy to demonstrate why that's not true.

Say you have a physical retail store selling office supplies, and you have 20,000 people come to your store in a month. If those 20,000 people are expecting to buy shoes, you're probably not going to get as many sales as you expect from those 20,000 people.

Some of the people looking for shoes might think that school will start again soon, and they should get some supplies. The majority, though, are going to come in and leave without buying anything.

You want *qualified* traffic. You want people who are interested in what you're doing, people coming to your website who are going to be good fits for you as clients.

Say you have 1,000 attorneys come to your website. If you're specifically a legal nurse consultant who deals primarily in neonatal care, and the attorneys who are coming to you are DWI specialists, that's still not a good fit. It's great that they are attorneys, but it's not within the field that you're looking for.

Always concentrate on qualifying traffic. With Facebook advertising, you can greatly narrow it down to that specific niche of the people that you're looking for. There are sources of paid traffic that are extremely cheap but that aren't targeted at all. You can get 100,000 people to your website, but they may be completely unrelated to anything that you can offer them.

Being Effective in Getting and *Keeping* Website Traffic

Traffic is not a once and done type of thing. You don't think, "Okay, this morning I wake up, I'm going to get my traffic, and then the rest of the week I can hunker down and do the work." Traffic is part of your sales funnel. (Chapter 14 *Nurturing Your Relationships with Prospects* gives more tips about sales funnels.) It's a process of getting people in and once they are in, you have all the work to follow up with them and develop the relationships.

Get traffic on a consistent basis to your website. When we talk about traffic, we're not just talking about cold traffic. That's another mistake people make. They always think traffic means *new* people coming to your website for the first time. *It's more cost effective to keep a current client or customer and sell them something else.* Having the repeat business from that person will cost you less to do than to acquire a brand-new customer with whom you have never worked.

Never forget your current base of clients and customers when you're thinking about additional work. You can put them in some sort of follow-up email series, send a newsletter or whatever your process is to let them know about additional things that you're doing.

You might start out with an attorney who just sends you a case and is only asking for your opinion. You can contact her later and say, "By the way, we also offer these additional services. We can testify for you. We can be the expert witness." List all the different types of services that you offer because if she's happy with what you've done for her in one capacity, there's a good chance that she is ready to hire you for something else.

Get Involved and Be Helpful

Another strategy that people sometime resist is to get involved in various online and offline groups or communities. Facebook has all kinds of groups. Chat forums are geared around specific topics. Go there, participate, and post and answer questions. You can have what's known as a signature line. It would include your name, your business, and your website.

That's a perfect place to do some really soft advertising because when you post your answers to people, when you help people, they are going to see that information. They may say, "Wow, that's really good information. Let me click on a link to find out what else they do."

This is a great way to get people back to your website. You're just helping people out. You're doing what you normally do, and the benefit is that you're getting that additional exposure.

As you do that online, you can also do that offline. Attend some events and do networking where your clients are going to be. (See Chapter 11, *Rebooting Your Marketing* for more information on creative networking.) Let them know about you and give them your card. Tell them that they can go to your website for more information. Always promote your website.

Make Sure Your Website Address is in Your Email

At the bottom of your email make sure you have your website address. Don't just sign it, "Thanks, Your Name." At the bottom of my email I have ways for people to contact me. I list my websites.

My emails look like this:

Pat Iyer

Phone number

www.patiyer.com - Pat's speaker site

www.LegalNursePodcasts.com - our new podcast exclusively for LNCs

www.LegalNurseBusiness.com - books and on demand and live online training for LNCs

www.LNCAcademy.com - coaching to help LNCs get more clients, earn more money and avoid expensive mistakes

www.LNCCEU.com - membership site for monthly online training for LNCs

In Conclusion

Basically, no matter what kind of promoting or marketing you're doing, think "Website, website, website." You want them to visit you where your business lives.

Key Points

- If you build your website, people will not come unless you promote your site.

- Tell people about your site.

- Consider using social media to drive traffic to your website.

- You may build traffic to your site slowly or more rapidly with ads.

- Be careful what you wish for. Be prepared to deal with an influx of work.

- Your goal is to get qualified traffic to your site.

- Work on consistently getting traffic to your site.

- It's more cost effective to keep a current client or customer and sell them something else.

- Get involved in online and offline networking groups.

CHAPTER 11

Rebooting Your Marketing

Do you feel stuck in your legal nurse consulting practice? Is it not growing as it needs to grow in order for you to make a good living?

Here are some possible reasons for why you're stuck.

- You may be unfocused.

- You may be doing too much low-fee work.

- You may be working for the wrong kinds of clients.

- You may be taking on the wrong kinds of cases.

This book is full of suggestions and recommendations for shifting gears in your business. In this chapter, I place particular emphasis on your website as an expression of your uniqueness as a legal nurse consultant. However, in order to take in and apply any strategies, you need to be very clear on who you are and what you do.

I know from my long experience as an LNC (and, more generally, as an entrepreneur) that before you can engage in clear thinking, you need a clear head. Here's how I get that clarity.

Breathe and Stop Criticizing Yourself

Everyone can benefit from taking several deep breaths when they feel stressed. Inhale, making sure that your abdomen is going out. Exhale, making sure that it's contracting. (This is the opposite of how most people breathe.) Do this several times. Oxygen is good for you.

After deep breathing, I would also recommend that you stop beating yourself up about all those things that seem to be going wrong. Give up self-criticism. End negative mind chatter. Stop trying to rewrite the past. Give up asking yourself why strategies that worked for other people don't work for you.

A shift to the positive will help you mentally, physically, spiritually, and psychologically to get re-centered and let go of some of the craziness that you may be experiencing in your business right now.

You *can* make the changes that are necessary. You can reboot your marketing, focus on your ideal client, start taking the revenue side of your business more seriously, or whatever has priority for you.

Focus on the many strategies you can adopt. Let's begin.

Distinguish Yourself From Other LNCs

Thousands of nurses have gone through courses to become legal nurse consultants. When they finish those courses, they prepare marketing materials that use the same language. Their marketing materials, letters, and websites *all* sound the same. How can a legal nurse consultant differentiate herself or himself from others? You can do this by finding your niche.

Learn the industry you want to focus on. Within law, there are attorneys who specialize in personal injury attorneys, medical malpractice, products liability and so on. There are insurance companies, law firms, or government agencies. Take a look at where you are and at what kinds of cases you like. If you enjoy working with a certain type of client, why not try to find those clients? If you focus in this way, every single time you wake up in the morning, you will be excited to go to work.

Who Do You Want to Reach?

Many legal nurse consultants use marketing language that is geared to medical malpractice attorneys, which is a quite small niche within the world of attorneys. The legal nurse consultants explain how they can screen cases for merit or research the standard of care. When that language is in marketing materials or on websites, it doesn't speak to the attorney who does *not* handle medical malpractice cases. I've had attorneys come up to me when I have exhibited who looked at my booth and said, "Oh, you're a legal nurse consultant. That means that you only do medical malpractice cases. I don't handle those." I then have to pivot and say, "What type of law do you practice? These are the things that we can do to help you with your cases."

Have Different Sections in Your Website

Your home page is the door of your website. You say, "I want to take these people in a certain direction." I would have a medical malpractice page. Direct a medical malpractice attorney to the medical malpractice page and then speak his or her language. Listen to your market. If your medical malpractice attorneys are specifically wanting something, don't paraphrase it. Tell them exactly what you can offer them by first listening to them.

You can have another section of your site for personal injury, long-term care litigation, or elder law. Your site doesn't have just one or two services pages.

Let's say there were three types of law practices you want to work with: medical malpractice, personal injury and products liability. Build a page for each type of practice. Share links to that specific page. It should have a contact form saying, "If you leave your name, email address and your phone number, we'll contact you for a personal phone call," or "Here's our phone number."

When somebody comes onto that particular page, for example a personal injury attorney, you're addressing everything that person needs. Why have them go anywhere else? There should be a clear call to action on every page, so that whether a lawyer is in medical malpractice, personal injury, toxic tort, or another specific industry, they can get what they want written in their language.

Learn to Listen to Your Ideal Client's Needs

Your approach needs to be in plain English. It needs to speak directly to the heart of a specific kind of buyer about their specific kind of problem. It's not marketing speak. It's not clever copy. This is more about copy *listening* than about copy *writing*.

Your clients and prospects are giving you information all the time. Think about and write down what they've told you about their complaints, problems, and frustrations. You should end up with 30 or 40. Pick the best 5 to 7. These are your 5 selling points that you can use as bulleted items.

Your goal is to have a prospect think, "This person really gets it. She's speaking my language."

The best compliment that you're going to get is someone calling you to say, "I was just on your website, and I felt like you were talking to me. That's exactly what we're going through, and that's exactly what we're up against. I wish I had found you three years ago. This is perfect."

That's the reaction that you want. Write your five bullets without clever copy writing or manipulative, sleazy techniques. Simply re-listen in your mind to all the folks that you've already worked with.

At the beginning of our legal nurse consulting businesses, we may spend a lot of wasted energy going after everyone. We create these opportunities and broadcast the message: "I serve the world," when in reality that's not true.

Get really clear about who your prospective client is, who gives you energy, who you enjoy working with, and start to target your messaging. That in itself starts to help you qualify your prospects to see if you are able to best serve them. I discuss qualifying prospects in more detail in *How to Get More Cases: Sales Secrets for Legal Nurse Consultants*. That's Book 6 in this series. (You may order it at **http://lnc.tips/Creatingseries**).

How are You Unique as a Legal Nurse Consultant?

When you put too much emphasis on the service you sell, you don't differentiate yourself from other legal nurse consultants. The prospect (potential client) who reads a list of your services may be saying, "Blah, blah, blah, I've read this a hundred times. What makes her stand out? What can she do for me?"

Let's say your marketing material says,

- "I locate expert witnesses"

- "I do summaries of medical records"

- "I analyze medical records"

"I, I, I" is the surest way to turn a prospect off. The attorney is concerned with his needs and what you can do for him.

Reduce selling to attorneys to the most basic level. Every legal nurse consultant is ultimately selling the same outcome of legal nurse consulting services: the results of what your service will do for the attorney. Attorneys buy what they get from your services:

- A well-qualified expert witness who can help her win her case

- A summary of a medical record that enables her to quickly locate details of injuries and treatment

- An analysis of records that highlights strengths and weaknesses of a case so that the attorney is not surprised

Usually, legal nurse consultants rely too much on a list of services and don't sell what attorneys really want to buy: what they *get* from the services.

Attorneys retain legal nurse consultants to help them with their cases because

- they are overwhelmed by medical records and afraid they will miss something.

- they are afraid that if they try to communicate with a potential expert, they may not be able to answer the expert's questions.

- they want a medical intermediary who can effectively communicate with healthcare providers.

They want to concentrate on the legal parts of the case and delegate the medical issues to the LNC.

What Is Important to Your Ideal Client?

In choosing a niche or niches, you must find out what is important to your ideal client. You'll see me refer to this a lot in this book.

Suppose your niche is personal injury attorneys. They're going to have a different need than healthcare law attorneys. The personal injury attorney needs help understanding injuries, pre-existing conditions, complications and permanency. They have a stack of medical records they don't understand and don't have time to go through.

When you address that need, the attorneys on your website realize, "Wow, this person really knows who I am."

There are two words that you really want to address with your website. When attorneys come to your website, you want them to feel *confident* that you are the one who can help them with whatever need they have. You then want them to feel *comfortable* in taking the next step, which is either picking up the phone, sending a brief email, or filling out a brief form to get you to call them back.

Make people feel confident in who you are and that you can address their needs so that they are comfortable making the next step. The next step is predetermined by the way the website is designed. Here are some essentials.

1. Your phone number is easy to find.

You have a form on the site that says, "Please contact us for a free analysis or a free phone call."

You can make them feel confident that you're *the one*, which makes them comfortable in that call to action. Then they will subconsciously take action. They will get on the site and say, "This person knows exactly what my needs are." They will then pick up the phone and call you. They will say, "I was on your website and I saw that you do work with personal injury attorneys. I felt very comfortable that I could call you and you would know exactly what I need."

You reply, "Yes, I do. I can help you with that." If the attorney asks about a service you do not list on the website, and you can provide it, it should be easy for you to get in and make the update. The next time somebody has that need, your answer is on your site.

2. Address the Attorneys' Pain Points

Consider these questions when you are writing content for your website.

"Are you suffering with this?"

"Are you frustrated about that?"

"Are you tired of this?"

"Do you want more of that?"

"Are you concerned about this?"

"Are you noticing more and more of this?"

"Are you hearing this in the hallway?"

"Are you seeing this in meetings?"

You give them a very personal experience of the fact that you *get* their problems. You're totally in sync with their heartaches, headaches, gaps, and challenges.

Here's something to contemplate. *"Experts win on a value and generalists die on a price."* You must be an expert in a fairly narrow niche. People who generally do what you do are a dime a dozen, but true *problem solvers* are priceless. You should position yourself as a problem solver.

The key to doing this successfully is clarity. Articulate clearly and powerfully that you can solve these kinds of problems. You'll win more points by being clear about how you define yourself and the confidence with which you do so.

Be specific and focused because there's no such thing as a general answer to a specific problem. People don't pay for *general* answers to their very *specific* problems. The main purpose of all of your marketing is to convey two ideas about your ideal client's needs.

- I know what you're going through.

- I can fix it.

3. Create Emotional Descriptions that Highlight the Results of Your Legal Nurse Consulting Services

Sales are made based on emotion. Here's a way to make clear the results of working with you. Sit down with a few of your clients and ask, "What value do I provide to you?" Ask about their emotions. How do they feel when they get reports from you?

Use this feedback to come up with descriptive words, terms, and phrases that help prospects to understand the results of working with you before they send you a case. Get the senses involved. Can they see, feel, touch, or hear the results of your services? If so, how?

Ask questions of your clients to get at the *emotional* benefits:

- "When you receive organized medical records back

from me, what do you see?"

- "How does it make you feel when I supply a really good expert?"

- "How do you feel when you read my analysis of cases?"

You may be delighted by what you hear. Or you may hear opportunities for improvement. When you put yourself in your client's position, you will be able to gather information to help you create images that evoke emotion. Help them understand the benefits of using your legal nurse consulting services. Don't talk about the services they get but rather what the benefits they will receive when they buy your services.

If possible, demonstrate how your legal nurse consulting services help the prospect. Tell stories; give examples. Seek to convey the emotions behind the story. Show the prospect how he can achieve the great feelings he wants when he works with you.

To Become an Expert, Go to the Experts

Another way to more clearly identify your clients' needs is to go to the experts. If, for example, you need to know more about workers' compensation, call an attorney who specializes in this field and say, "I was wondering if you could help me." You say, "I'm a legal nurse consultant and I have a lot of experience, but I'm very interested in finding out how my expertise could help you in product liability cases." Then listen to them explain exactly how they would use somebody like you or why they would need somebody like you. You can take that information and turn it into either a marketing brochure, a piece on your website, or as a way to introduce yourself to another products liability lawyer.

Also, consider hiring an expert coach - an LNC who has built a successful LNC business. Many try to succeed in this business – not all succeed. Interested in talking with me about your LNC business? Check out this link. http://lnc.tips/Consult

Niche Call Days

Let's say you are making cold calls to attorneys. One way to make the process easier is to set aside a "niche day". On this day, you will call lawyers in one of the niches you've chosen. By the time you make the fourth or fifth call in that niche, you've collected information from the attorneys you reached. Everybody who you talked has given you information you can use on the next call. Instead of sitting down here and saying, "I need to call a medical malpractice attorney, I need to call a personal injury attorney", focus on a niche, pick a niche, learn that niche, call that niche, and talk to people. If that niche becomes something that you really want to focus on, build a page for it on your website.

Making Your Website Reflect Who You Are

You don't want to have to pay someone else for every single word that has to be added to it. Be able to easily change your website as a reflection of your business. Learn how to make changes. You should have control over your site because your site should be ever-evolving. If you suddenly decide that you want to get into employment discrimination work, and there's not a section on your website for that, you should be able to go in and add it. Refer to Chapter 8, *Wonderful WordPress Websites* on the necessity for being able to modify your site.

Thinking Out of the Box

Think of ways to go where lawyers are. It could be a bar meeting or other attorney membership event. Use your imagination to figure out where lawyers might gather. This will probably be unique to your area. If your thinking is creative enough, you'll discover that other LNCs haven't used their imagination the way you did, and you may be the only player in the field.

Introduce yourself. Say, "I'm a nurse legal consultant, and I have a specialty in workers' compensation cases." They may ask what lawyers you've worked with. If you're fortunate, they'll know the names you share. Say that you're at the meeting to add to your expertise. You're not overtly trying to sell them. You're not handing them your business card. You want to learn. Attorneys will ask for your card if they are interested.

If you are at a lunch where people introduce themselves at the table, you repeat this message: you want to learn more about this industry and especially how you can help lawyers in this field. You might not meet the actual decision makers, but you may get the names of people who are.

In addition, you're showing your interest in their area of law. They'll be flattered that you want to hear their expertise. People like to be helpful, and it's a plus if they also get to show what they know.

Dealing with Cost Questions

A lot of attorneys ask about price the minute that they pick up the phone. How it's often manifested is: "I have a pile of medical records sitting in front of me. How much is it going to cost for you to go through them?"

At times I've wanted to say (but never have), "Let's see. If this was a camera phone, and I could look at the medical records . . . I need to know how are they organized, are they not organized, are they handwritten or are they typed, how many inches do you have, what type of services do you need?" It's almost an impossible question to answer.

If the attorney is not local, respond by asking for the records and a retainer, and then provide an estimate once you have seen the records.

If the attorney is local, I'd say I can't estimate the stack of files the lawyer has, and I ask if we could get together for 15 or 20 minutes. Try this. Say, "Can we get together next Tuesday? I'm estimating this might take 12 minutes, 22 minutes or 24 minutes." They then say, "24 minutes? A little bit less than 30 minutes and more than 20 minutes. Sure."

You bill by the hour or by the minute. If you said something like that, they would probably say, "Okay that's fine." When you enter the attorney's office your appointment will never be exactly 18 minutes. You want to be totally authentic. When the 18 minutes are up, you say, "When we initially talked, I said that I would talk with you for 18 minutes, but is it okay if we continue?" Then you've got them. They will say, "Yes, it's okay if we continue."

The approach may be slightly different if someone were to call and ask, "How much are your services?" without naming a specific need. I would say something like, "Can we talk about exactly the type of case you have?" "I'm a medical malpractice attorney." "Great, I've worked with other medical malpractice attorneys. What type of case or what type of services do you need help with?"

Are you going to be *confident* in who you are and then be *comfortable* in taking the next step? In either case, I recommend saying, "Why don't we get together and talk about it more?"

Don't Chase Business

Don't chase business, no matter how desperate you are to make a sale, because it comes across that way on the phone, and then people can take advantage of you. They may think, "Well, you need this sale, so I bet you will negotiate your fee." You need to project, "No, I don't need the sale because I'm an expert in my field, and you need me."

Don't come off cocky; come off as an *expert*. They're calling you because you are the expert. They should pay the expert fees because you differentiated yourself by asking questions that show you're unlike the 40 other legal nurse consultants who they called.

They called you. If they called you, there's a reason. You don't know if it's because they found the website, got a referral, or heard about you from somebody else whom they work with, but they're calling you. That's a captive audience, and you want to keep that audience. The last thing that you want to do is immediately discount your fee.

How to Get More Cases: Sales Secrets for Legal Nurse Consultants is devoted to the topic of closing sales. Get your copy at **http://lnc.tips/Creatingseries**.

Pay Attention and Take Notes

I keep notepads by me for every time I take a call. An attorney may use a term or concept I don't know. I write it down and say, "Look, I will be honest with you. I have a lot of experience as a legal nurse consultant, but I'm not familiar with that exact term. I would like to do a little research on it. Could you help me and give me a little bit more explanation about exactly what you were looking for?"

Or you could say, "I've worked with other malpractice attorneys before, but something that you're asking about I just need a little bit more clarification on." Write down whatever they say, and then look for those particular terms. You say, "Thank you. Yes, I know exactly what you're talking about now."

You're looking for the particular terms in that related industry. Once you know them, you can say to another attorney, "In my experience, this has come up." When you talk specifically their language, you suddenly become an authority.

In summary, you listen to the people who are in that particular industry or that particular target market and then repeat back exactly what they have said for other people in that market. They can basically feel like they're the authority, and I think that's what people want.

You Can't Hire Out the Sales Work

I tried to encourage somebody in my company to act as a sales person. It was always a challenge because the employees who love to do medical record reviews are not necessarily the same people who like to go out and make sales calls.

I considered having a retired attorney act as a marketing person for me. I spoke to a couple of retired attorneys, and neither one of them was particularly interested in the role. In exploring this with some other small business owners, I learned you need technical expertise, as well as marketing skills and that mindset, and sales skills.

I learned that I was the best salesperson for my company because I had a passion for what I did and also because I could draw from years of experience. I had the most comprehensive answer to the question: "What's a legal nurse consultant?" I could also answer it in a way that allowed me to differentiate myself from other LNCs.

Making the "Hello" Calls

That said, I understand the difficulty most people have in making sales calls. You can soften this fear by looking at these calls as the process of developing a relationship.

One way to do this is to make a friendly call. Have you ever picked up the phone and called somebody and said, "Hi, I just wanted to see how you were doing" without trying to sell them something?

You could call up and say, "Hey, I was concerned about you. I wanted to see how you were doing". The call is to find out how people are doing. This can also happen with "Hello Texts." You could text someone and say, "Hey, I was thinking about you. I'm at a restaurant where we used eat. I wanted to see how you were doing." This can warm up a relationship.

No one wants to be sold, but they want to buy. All you're trying to do is make a relationship with somebody, and from that foundation you can start talking a little bit more about what you do. Say, "I do such-and-such for the people that I work with." Differentiate yourself.

You want conversations and relationships rather than a feeling of needing to be a high pressure salesperson. There are so many adjectives that people attach to salesperson. Sleaze, as I've said elsewhere in this book, is associated with sales, which immediately makes everyone get on the defensive. *How to Get More Cases: Sales Secrets for Legal Nurse Consultants* for an entire book on the topic of closing sales. You can order it at this link **http://lnc.tips/Creatingseries**

Other Ways to Show You Care

When you're reading the paper or scanning Facebook, you might see a topic that would interest one of your clients.

You can send a link or take a photo of the headline and send it to him or her. This isn't anything like, "Oh, by the way, we can help you market to that opportunity." It's, "Hey, I was thinking about you."

That's the relationship that you want. I guarantee you that the attorneys you're working for are getting calls from other legal nurse consultants trying to get business. All you want to do is keep the business without trying to sell them every time you talk to them.

In Conclusion

You're still breathing, right? I hope that now you have a fresh perspective on your business. Why not pick out one of the ideas in this chapter and start working on it? I think you'll discover that this will open doors for you.

Key Points

- Look at why you might be stuck in your business.

- Breathe and stop criticizing yourself. Stop trying to rewrite the past.

- Distinguish yourself from other LNCs.

- Use your website to address the interests of various types of attorneys.

- Listen to your ideal client's needs.

- Focus on your uniqueness as an LNC.

- Make visitors to your website feel confident and comfortable that you are the right person for them.

- Make it easy for attorneys to reach you.

- Use your website to address the attorney's pain points. Create emotional descriptions that highlight the results of your legal nurse consulting services.

- Research your field by talking to experts.

- It is imperative that you be in control of your website so you can easily make changes. Make the site reflective of your services and who you are.

- Use your imagination to locate places where attorneys gather.

- Project confidence and that you do not need to make a sale.

- Make "hello calls and "hello texts" to clients.

- No one wants to be sold, but they want to buy.

CHAPTER 12

The Power of Marketing with Social Media

Stripped apart, the term "social media" has two different pieces you'll need to understand: the social aspect and the media aspect. Most people know that the term "social" refers to interaction with others, including developing relationships and cultivating new connections. The term "media," in this instance, refers to the way social information is exchanged.

There are literally hundreds of social media networks. You could spend a lifetime developing profiles and engaging with connections both old and new on these networks. As an entrepreneur, though, you need social media in order to present yourself in a certain way to legal professionals, as well as to help you make connections that allow you to succeed as a legal nurse consultant.

Who Can Use Social Media?

Whether or not you're currently using social media in a personal capacity, or you are trying to make a legal nurse consulting business profile, there's no better time than the present to jump on the social media bandwagon. You can rest assured that your competitors have already considered the importance of social media and networking, and may have already created profiles on various social media networks.

The longer you wait to create profiles and begin to develop business connections, the more behind the times you'll find yourself. It's important to utilize social media because it's 100% free, far-reaching, and effective in developing a stronger client base. You'll see the value of social media once you learn to effectively brand yourself professionally.

How Can Social Media Benefit Your Business?

Other forms of digital or print marketing may cost you hundreds or even thousands of dollars to execute, while pretty much 100% of the basic functions of any social media network come at no cost. Social media can serve as incredibly effective, cheap marketing for your legal nurse consulting business.

Social media also allows you to reach a new audience like never before. While your ambitions may not include interacting with professionals in other countries, social media gives you the ability to do so if you desire. Using this type of marketing, you're able to reach out to folks who would have been impossible to connect with 20 years ago. In addition, you have the capacity to vastly increase your social network within your own country or even your local area.

Just a few hours a day using social media tools will result in connections you never thought possible. Regardless of whether or not those connections are down the street or across the globe, you never know who you're going to meet, or what effect your new connections will have on your legal professional networking.

Direct Marketing

What about the things social media can't do? Many people using social media make the mistake of expecting direct marketing relationships or sales to result. Direct marketing is a way to reach customers that will result directly in a sale. Many people expect that they're going to go out, create social media profiles, and begin selling their services immediately online.

Unfortunately, social media marketing isn't a direct sales marketing technique. If you're becoming involved in social media, patience should be your first virtue. Social media marketing is all about establishing relationships and developing connections with potential clients. For you, this means social media networking is going to serve as a way for people seeking your services to find out more about you, learn about the services you offer and what your business is like, and even see testimonials or interactions with previous legal professionals who have been happy with your services. You're not necessarily looking for a lawyer to view your social media profiles or Facebook business page and get so excited about what you do that he or she contacts you and immediately engages you in business. In an ideal world, this would be the result – but social media doesn't work that way.

What you are looking for is efficient and low-cost branding that will make you look like you know what you're doing.

If a social media profile seems too simplistic a method of displaying that information, you're not really thinking about social media the right way. It's important to learn how to develop that sort of on-point advertising for yourself without expecting a direct sale.

Follow these guidelines for using social media.

Traditional ethic rules apply. Do not share information about cases that are in suit or have a confidentiality agreement in place about the verdict. In some cases, neither the amount awarded nor the names of the plaintiffs or defendants may be released. Your attorney client is the best source of knowledge about whether you can share this information.

Assume everything you write online will become public, potentially in an embarrassing way. This is true even in it is on an account that is not explicitly linked to your employer. Think of it this way: How would your social media message look on a billboard for all to see? A man on his way to a meeting with Fed Ex executives tweeted disparaging remarks about Fed Ex's hometown. His tweet got to the conference room before he did. He was greeted with frosty expressions.

Don't post embarrassing photographs on Facebook. An attorney who plans to hire you will likely have checked you out on Facebook before that crucial interview or contact with you. I know an expert witness who posted a picture of herself in a bar holding a beer bottle and exposing her bra strap. Imagine that showing up in a courtroom the next time the expert testified? She took the photo off after

I talked to her. I am aware of a story of a man who posted that he was at a party when he actually called in sick. He lost his job. Another man posted pictures of his trip with his mistress. His wife was not amused.

Engage with readers professionally. Interact with others and respond to messages. Check to see if you are being mentioned on Twitter and thank people who retweet your messages. Respond to people who comment about your Linkedin or Facebook messages.

Break news on your website, not on Twitter. The purpose of announcements and press releases is to drive traffic to your site. You can tweet a link to your announcement on your site.

Spread the potential reach of your tweets or Facebook postings by mentioning another person. When you do that, your message will go to your followers or friends and also to that other person's following (if you are friends on Facebook.)

Social networks are tools, not toys. Cite a source when you are passing on information. Give credit to bloggers or article postings.

Be transparent and correct mistakes when you make them. Be quick to offer new information if it challenges what you have written.

Make sure your LinkedIn profile contains nothing but the truth. If you misrepresent your work history, you'll be found out. Employers and potential clients are looking at your profile before you even walk in the door.

In Conclusion

Use the power of social media to make connections, share news. Be discreet about what you share.

Key Points

- There are hundreds of social media networks.

- The longer you wait to create profiles and begin to develop business connections, the more behind the times you'll find yourself.

- Many people using social media make the mistake of expecting direct marketing relationships or sales to result.

- Do not share information about cases that are in suit or have a confidentiality agreement in place about the verdict.

- Assume everything you write online will become public, potentially in an embarrassing way.

- Don't post embarrassing photographs on Facebook.

CHAPTER 13

Increase Your Visibility

Yes, *you* need online marketing skills. Success as a legal nurse consultant is achieved with a combination of clinical knowledge, business experience, and online marketing skills. It is not enough to excel in one of these areas.

Online marketing skills, oddly enough, are often the one element that causes legal nurse consultants to turn and run away. It feels overwhelming and insurmountable. But you shouldn't feel like you have to be able to operate everything all at once – don't make this harder than it has to be.

Even if you have the money to outsource most of your marketing needs, it's imperative that you know a bit about what's happening. That way, when you outsource, you'll know if you're getting your money's worth and if what you requested is actually what you're receiving.

Get specific tips on how to outsource in *How to Manage Your LNC Business and Clients*: *Top Tips for Success*, part of the **Creating a Successful LNC Practice** series. Get it at this **link: http://lnc.tips/Creatingseries**.

Other things you might think you need to outsource are really very simple and only require a few minutes to learn.

There are so many ways to get the help you need to perform some of the technical skills in online marketing that will make you successful. I have gone to countless online marketing seminars and taken courses to understand how to more effectively market my businesses online.

The learning process is never over if you're an entrepreneur. There are some specific basics you need to know so you'll understand how to perform some of the online marketing techniques that are vital to your success. Let's take a peek at some of the necessary skills you should look into.

Master social media's ins and outs. Social media sites have technical aspects you need to understand if you're to make a success of your online business. Most are little nuances that simply add to the social media experience. These are part of your marketing and public relations efforts.

The difference between marketing and public relations is a subtle one. When you market, you're bringing a service to the attention of those who want and need it. Public relations is more indirect. You're communicating a message from a client (who in this case is you) to the media.

The media are interested in a story. In other words, what you communicate has to be newsworthy. Ask yourself how what *you* do can be a newsworthy story. (For the actual crafting of that story, you can get a lot of help from Section Three: *Marketing with Stories*.)

Your Target Market

While media consultants say that reaching your target market hasn't become *more* difficult in the past ten to fifteen years, the *methods* have changed. It's a lot easier to be online and get visibility today then it was 15 years ago because of all the social media, the Internet, Google, social media platforms, and email marketing.

The Role of Press Releases

You used to have to send out press releases one at a time by fax. You had to be very selective in choosing the targets. Now you can email them en masse or you can pay a distribution company under $100 to have 500 guaranteed placements, which doesn't include social media and other places where people can see your press release. A distribution company will send you a report that shows exactly where your press release was published. You can click on those and see the press release. Then you can share it, which gives it further exposure.

However, you could have 500 placements in media whose readers could care less about legal nurse consulting. You still have to target. Know where your potential audience is. With all the data mining that goes on today with Facebook, Google, and other resources, you have the opportunity to learn that.

In the past, small business owners would pray that the press release went to people who would be interested in publishing it in their newspaper. Now, although you might get a newspaper story, a press release does more for your search capabilities.

Increased visibility is the goal behind issuing press releases.

Specific Applications for LNCs

You know your target market is primarily attorneys who are handling cases involving medical issues. The first thing a well-connected attorney may do is to ask a colleague, "Who have you used?" Or the attorney may go on an attorney listserv and ask, "Who do you recommend?" If that inquiry didn't provide likely prospects, they would most likely do a search looking for the website of a legal nurse consultant.

One thing you can do, if you're not a member, is to join the American Association of Legal Nurse Consultants (AALNC). I was president of that association for a year. Its site has a directory, and once you're a member, you can have your business listed in the directory. The directory is accessible to people who are not members of the association, such as attorneys, as well as other members of the association.

I recommend that when you join, you make your AALNC membership prominent on your web site. It gives you greater credibility. You can also make an announcement of this in press releases.

Subjects that could be worthy of a press release might include the launching or anniversary of your business, a new book you've written, or other accomplishments, or trends in legal nursing.

Social Media

As you read in Chapter 3, *Relationship Marketing: Developing the Know, Like, and Trust,* social media is all about building relationships. See with whom you can have useful relationships on Facebook, Twitter, and LinkedIn. Follow them and look to see who is writing about legal nurse material.

Build that relationship so they know who you are. Writers are always looking for someone to interview or for what's the latest thing going on in your field. They're going to call or contact someone they know or someone they know of.

Assemble names of those prominent in our industry. Follow them on Twitter, and go to their Twitter pages, which will show you their tweets. Look for five or six tweets you think are valuable. Like and re-tweet them with a comment, for example, "Thank you, Pat Iyer, for this great information. I look forward to getting to know you."

People you mention in this way will see in their messaging or their notifications that you mentioned them. Wait a few days and do it again. If you see a tweet from them, like it automatically.

Then like their Facebook page. Comment on that page as well in the same way.

Lots of videos and tutorials exist about how to take the most advantage of social media sites such as FaceBook and Linkedin.

LinkedIn

LinkedIn is especially useful in our field. When you're looking for whom to connect with on LinkedIn, look for the people you know who would someday need a legal nurse consultant. You can search for legal or use the term attorney or at least use the term lawyer if you know the person is a lawyer.

Send a connection request. You can follow them, you can mention them, and you can see what they're doing and what they're saying. You can then share this for other people to see.

If someone follows you, always send them an individualized note back saying "Thank you for following me. I look forward to connecting with you."

Build these kinds of relationships, and you will find your visibility increasing.

In my experience, LinkedIn should be a priority for any legal nurse consultant. I have found consulting work and met new clients through LinkedIn. If you are like me, the prospect of cold call marketing leaves you a little...cold. How can you market yourself to potential clients in a professional manner without being intrusive? How can you find clients that need the particular service you have to offer? How can you find like-minded individuals who can introduce you to individual attorneys and law firms all around the globe?

Edit your profile as often as you like, at no charge. Join groups that are likely to have members who can utilize your services, and add them to your personal connections. You can link to your personal website, blog, or any Internet-based enterprise that you want to promote.

Do you want to be seen as an authority in your area of expertise? Set up your profile so that new discussions and questions from your group come into your email as they arise. Too much email? Change your preferences to group this data on a daily or weekly basis.

Facebook and Twitter are wonderful social media tools, but too often the communication is of a personal nature that is not well suited to making serious business connections. However, LinkedIn is designed to work with all major social media markets. Tweet a news article and benefit from both markets.

With LinkedIn, you can update all your connections effortlessly. Are you teaching or attending a seminar? Post this as a discussion so that all will know instantly what you are up to. Do you have a networking event for your association that would interest your contacts? Announce that event and your contact information under Discussions. Have you read an interesting article on a medical condition, a relevant jury decision, or a change in the law? Post it.

Use LinkedIn to find expert witnesses in any area – medical, dental, nursing, environmental, engineering – there is one (and usually more) specialty group for any expertise.

Instead of emailing your resume and achievements to new prospects, send them a link to your profile.

Have you done exceptionally good work for an attorney or other referral source? Ask them for a recommendation that will be publicly posted on your profile. In return, make a recommendation for that person – this benefits both of your practices.

Would you like to know when your contacts change jobs or move to a different firm? LinkedIn will tell you automatically. Have they announced a favorable decision in court, written a compelling blog or article, or voiced opinions on topics that you can relate to? Think of the opportunities you are missing without even knowing it.

Joining LinkedIn, creating a profile, and growing your network is free. As new nurses to the business world, we often ask ourselves, "How can I afford to have business cards, get another phone line, buy copiers, printers, scanners, fax machines, send out brochures, and everything else I need to start this new business of mine?" With LinkedIn, the only question is, "How can you afford not to?"

Be aware that Microsoft recently purchased LinkedIn. Some of the features you could use for free may be accessible only for a fee.

In Conclusion

Marketing is so much more than telling people about you. Frankly, they would rather hear you talk about *them.* Instead of asking bland and blind questions, read someone's profile and background. Communicate to them that you have invested time in them as individuals, and make the contact count by jumpstarting conversations with personal knowledge.

Key Points

- Success as a legal nurse consultant is achieved with a combination of clinical knowledge, business experience, and online marketing skills. It is not enough to excel in one of these areas.

- There are so many ways to get the help you need to perform some of the technical skills in online marketing that will make you successful.

- When you market, you're bringing a service to the attention of those who want and need it. Public relations is more indirect.

- Increased visibility is the goal behind issuing press releases.

- Make your AALNC membership prominent on your web site. It gives you greater credibility.

- Build relationships with others by following them on social media, liking their posts, and retweeting them.

- LinkedIn is a priority for connecting with others.

CHAPTER 14

Nurturing Your Relationships with Prospects

In today's digital world clients are in control of their buying experience. People want to feel as if *they* have found you and made the decision to work with you. As a business owner, you want to make a marketing program where you showcase the value of your company so that the client comes to you rather than you having to chase the client. In marketing speak, this is called "Inbound vs. Outbound Marketing."

Inbound marketing is a technique for drawing attorney clients to your services via content marketing, social media marketing, and search engine optimization.

Outbound marketing involves using techniques to become more visible through exhibiting, cold calls, email blasts, print and television ads.

There's a lot of content on websites, social media posts, and video sites. By giving something of value to your client, you can build a relationship with them and do what we call "Pull vs. Push Marketing." You want to become the *hunted*, not the *hunter*. Make yourself so valuable and so desirable that people want to do business with you.

Ten years ago we were just getting started with Facebook, and now it's a marketing powerhouse. You can reach thousands of people for very low advertising prices right now. That's exciting if you do it right. (I went into more detail about Facebook advertising in Chapter 10, *Secrets of Driving Traffic to Your Website*.)

Email Marketing

Email marketing is most manageable when you use a mailing service such as GetResponse, Aweber, Constant Contact, and others. You will need a service like this in order to send out more than a handful of emails at one time. Otherwise, your email server will flag the groups of messages as spam. Email marketing is one of the best way legal nurse consultants can build trust and to demonstrate expertise. Use it to give away things like free samples or free reports. Free videos are great. Provide little two-to-three minute videos about your business.

Your videos could present why you love being a legal nurse consultant. You could talk about a case (being careful to obscure details and names) and convey the gratification the verdict gave you. Describe how much you enjoy helping lawyers.

Presentations are great, as are webcasts or webinars. Free advice is very popular. Create a once-a-week advice column you send out to your list. Disseminate relevant content your clients would be interested in. (See how I share content with LNCs getting my free report and weekly ezine. Go to this link. http://lnc.tips/5Surefire)

The more relevant the free material is to your clients, the more likely they are to be engaged in and actually pay attention in this world of information overload. As an analogy, if you're a pet store marketing cat products to people who only like dogs, you're not probably going to be very successful. If you understand your client and you know what they want, if they're cat people, you want to send them cat stuff. You can do that with digital marketing today.

In the legal nurse consulting world there are many who put out websites or brochures that talk about helping attorneys identify standards of care, which is a term that medical malpractice attorneys are very interested in. That term is *not* interesting to attorneys who handle car accident cases or workers compensation injuries.

Using Social Media

There are so many social media channels today that it can start to get confusing. Experts I've asked say the top social media channels for businesses are Facebook, Twitter, YouTube, and LinkedIn.

Facebook. This is by far the biggest, with 1.3 billion daily active users or 72% of adult Internet users. Seventy eight percent of Facebook users say they use Facebook for professional purposes. They might not have professional websites. Maybe they're on Facebook to see what's going on with their friends. If you're putting an ad up that appeals to attorneys, even though they might not be on there for professional purposes at the time, that's still their profession, and they will still take notice.

Facebook definitely gets the most engaged user base, with people logging on and off several times a day. Advertising on Facebook is relatively cheap right now. For something like $150 you can reach somewhere in the range of at least 5,000 people.

Twitter: Only 23% of adult Internet users are on Twitter. That's still 313 million monthly active users. Consumption of content and reading on Twitter is steadily increasing, but I would say if you were going to choose between the two, start with Facebook, and make Twitter your second choice.

LinkedIn: If you are a business-to-business client, which legal nurses consultants would be, LinkedIn is also a good channel. In fact 46% of college graduates are using LinkedIn. LinkedIn is a great place to be not only for business but for staying connected to contacts and colleagues, especially clients. You can find new clients on LinkedIn.

People are often concerned about accepting a connection request. They think, "I don't know if I really know this person, but they have asked to connect to me on LinkedIn." More often than not, it's a good idea to connect to them as long as they look like they are a legitimate business person. You can actually find more people or be connected to more people based on the people in your network. The more first level connections you have, the more second level connections you can reach out to.

There's a whole strategy behind using LinkedIn to ask people who are your first level connections to introduce you to, for example, an attorney whom you are attempting to reach. You can get better visibility with LinkedIn by sharing blog posts on the timeline or as LinkedIn articles. You can be active in LinkedIn groups by making comments, offering information or sharing opinions. They are all ways that people on LinkedIn can get to know you better.

I have a LinkedIn marketing group that I run called "Legal Nurse Consultant Marketing." It's a great way to ask questions or share information about your perspective as a legal nurse consultant. (Please see Chapter 13, *How to Increase Your Visibility*, for more detailed information about LinkedIn.)

YouTube: YouTube is by far the most lucrative social media channel for businesses, but for some reason a lot of businesses are not on YouTube. In fact, only 38% of self-employed business owners use YouTube for marketing purposes.

YouTube is *huge*. It has over a billion active users, or 1/3 of all people using the Internet. Four times as many clients would rather be watching a video about a product then actually reading about it. Almost 50% of Internet users look for video related to a product or service before actually visiting a store for that product.

We all know that in today's world video is huge. People want to see video. Many people would rather watch a video than read text; video is also very personal. You can connect with people over video.

Consider building a YouTube channel for marketing. Suppose you have 20 two-to-three minute videos with tips or tidbits that would be important or interesting to your clients. People are watching those videos, and people are going to feel like they know you. You may not even know them, but they feel like they know you because they have been listening to you and watching you for some time. I've had the experience of LNCs meeting me in person after they have seen my YouTube videos on my LegalNurseBusiness channel. They greet me like a friend.

Video is a great tool, and there are a couple of online services that you can use to help you make videos, including Animoto. This is a marketing video service that you can subscribe to. It gives you a format for you to upload photos and videos, and put text and music with it. That would be helpful if you're getting started and don't really know how to make a professional video.

As an alternative, use your phone, an iPhone or whatever device you have. Film yourself. The cameras in today's smartphones are good. You don't need a heavy video camera mounted on a tripod anymore. As long as you've got good sound with an external mic, you can do a quick video and post that on YouTube. If you wish, add some photos, some texts and music, and make it exciting.

What do you create a video about? You can Google topics related to your business and see what people are searching for. When you get a feeling for what kinds of topics are already being searched for, you can create your videos around those topics. You'll be making them about something with high search relevance.

Think about the topics that you can demonstrate your expertise on. You can take a blog that you've written and turn that into a video with a camera that's trained on you.

Use those videos to gain attention, to bring people to your website, and to invite them to sign up for your free reports so you can stay in touch with them.

Google+: Make yourself a Google+ account. You can register your business with your phone number, business address, and business name. When people search on Google, they will find you there. When you create your YouTube channel through Google+, every time you upload a video, it immediately populates to your Google+.

Avoid These Mistakes

A lot of people tend to be focused on their website. They think that they need to have a great website, and they *do* need this. Focus on driving more traffic to their website. (See Chapter 10, *Secrets of Driving Traffic to Your Website*, for details on this topic.) While website traffic is a good thing, it's not your *only* strategy. Overall, focus your efforts on generating more leads so that you can make more sales. You need additional methods for doing this.

Imagine that you're having a garage sale. You want to make sure people drive down your street so that they will stop and buy. You put signs up on the main street. You put signs up on the street corner so that the drivers know where to turn. But when they get to your house, your garage sale is set up in the backyard, and you forgot to put a sign out front.

People might drive by, but they will quickly leave because they haven't found what they're looking for. This is a common problem with a lot of businesses owners who are trying to do their marketing online. People want to drive traffic to their website, but the problem is when a person gets to your website, there's too many distracting features. There are so many different pages. There is often not a really solid, clear call to action. Maybe there are multiple calls to action, and the person might lose interest and get lost.

Actually 55% of visitors spend less than 15 seconds on the average website. If a person gets to your website, and there are a lot of different messages, in 15 seconds they are likely not going to figure out what they should do. They don't come back. They don't actually do anything while they are there, and you've lost them. That's a really big problem, but the good news is that you can solve it. There are ways of capturing that person's attention.

Today the website for your business is a brochure. It's not the place where you're going to get business. It's the place that's going to give you credibility if you meet somebody at a tradeshow or out at a networking event, for example. They don't really know what you're about, who you are, and if you're the right person for them yet.

Have a mobile friendly website. Many older LNC websites do not meet this criteria. About 75% of web searches are now done using a mobile device. If your website isn't mobile friendly, it will be harder to read. Google will penalize you for not redesigning your site to be mobile friendly. This is particularly a problem with older websites that were designed before mobile responsive themes became readily available. They don't resize to fit the phone.

I would encourage you to open your website on your cell phone and take a look at how it appears. If it's not reforming, reshaping, and compressing itself to fit the screen of a mobile phone, then it's time to get a new website.

What is a "Sales Funnel"?

Here are the stages that a client goes through when considering to do business with you. She asks:

1. Who are you?
   - In this stage, the client simply knows you exist.

2. What are you?
   - The client now knows you exist and what you do.

3. What about you? What do I think or feel about you?
   - The client is forming an opinion about you.

4. What about you and me? What is our connection?
   - In this stage, the client knows you exist. She knows what you are and what you do. She has an opinion about you.

These are always the steps that somebody goes through. For example, do you know anyone who would marry somebody without ever having been on a date with them? Probably not, and it's the same for your clients. They want to know you first. First, they have to know you exist. They can't do business with you if they don't even know you exist. They want to understand what you're about and then decide if you're the right solution for them. They have to do that before they can actually make a decision to do business with you.

As you can see, there are quite a number of steps to go through to decide if you're going to do business with somebody. If you're only having interactions with a person one time, that's not enough for them to go through those stages and understand if you're the right person or the right solution for them if they should do business with you.

A "Sales Funnel" is basically a system for taking your leads through this process to build a relationship with them from simply knowing you exist to knowing what you do, deciding to become a client, and then hopefully a *raving fan*. In building a sales funnel, the most important thing to start with is to understand who you best serve.

- Who is your ideal client?

- What are their interests?

- How old are they?

- Where do they live?

- Are they male or female, or maybe you appeal to both male and female?

Drill down and be very specific. You can create targeted online ads on platforms such as Facebook or Google. The more you can target, the better. If you're too broad, people are going to not pay attention. You might worry that you're going to alienate some people, but in marketing "If you're not talking to someone, you're talking to no one."

Consider creating a targeted Facebook or Google ad in which you can give a very specific message and then direct people who click on the ad to a targeted landing page. This is not your website home page. This is a specific page with a very specific purpose. It will have the same message as the ad that the person came from.

For your business, it might say, "Get my top 20 suggestions for winning your malpractice suits" (or nursing home or worker's comp). It could say, "What do you need to know about legal nurse consultants?" or "How can a legal nurse consultant help to streamline your business?"

If they click that link, it goes to a page that repeats the topic. Then it might say, "Enter your first name and email address. I'll send you my 20-page free guide on (topic you choose)."

Somebody might say, "I really need to figure out how to do that. Let me get her free guide." Then they give you their email address. Your mailing system immediately sends them that free report, and now you can periodically follow up with them by email. It takes five to eight touches before a person will actually take action. If you're trying to get them to buy something, if you're trying to get them to call you, they're not probably going to do that before they have received five to eight emails from you.

You would think people would simply buy whatever they need from you, but if they don't know who you are, they don't know what you do, and they won't buy. If they don't have an opinion about you or an opinion about what their relationship is with you, they won't be inclined to take action. If you would like more support in how to create this type of free report, get my personal assistance by joining my coaching program called *How to Create an Irresistible Opt In Offer.* See the details at this link. http://lnc.tips/CreateOptins

In Conclusion

"Email Nurturing" is possible after you first build your list, and that's what Facebook ads and the landing page help you to do. Nurture people into clients and that's what the repetitive emails do.

You don't want to be sending material people are not interested in. Make sure what you're sending is valuable. In fact, send things that you would normally sell. If you would normally sell a 20-page guide on legal nurse issues, give that away for free. The more value you can give to people, the more they're going to be interested in having a relationship with you and doing business with you.

Key Points

- Inbound marketing involves techniques to attract people to you.

- Outbound marketing involves becoming more visible through a variety of techniques.

- You want to become the hunted, not the hunter. Make yourself so valuable and so desirable that attorneys want to do business with you.

- Provide content in several formats to send out to your list of clients and prospects.

- The more relevant the free material is to your customers, the more likely they are to be engaged and actually pay attention.

- The top social media channels for businesses are Facebook, Twitter, YouTube, and LinkedIn. Facebook is the largest channel. Linkedin is a good channel for business to business contacts.

- Don't overlook the usefulness of YouTube as a marketing tool.

- Driving traffic to your website is important but not the only marketing strategy to use.

- A sales funnel has stages that define the client's awareness of your services.

- Define your ideal clients so you understand who you best serve.

- Use email sequences to nurture clients.

SECTION THREE

Marketing with Stories

CHAPTER 15

Content Marketing with Stories

Online business has many aspects. One of the most important is to create stories and to do a lot of research. As a legal nurse consultants, you know how to do research. You'll find it valuable to learn how to create more stories.

Every case with medical issues has a story. You may immediately think about personal injury and medical malpractice cases, but every type of litigation has stories.

The defective product that an uninformed consumer uses is a story. When a factory pumps toxic chemicals into the air for 25 years, and a person ends up living in a neighborhood where there is a very high rate of lung cancer, that's a compelling story. So is the narrative about a CEO who knows that a drug is potentially defective but who, because of the money invested in pumping a new drug out onto the market, has a powerful incentive to hide those results.

Everything, when told in an engaging way, is a story. In the newspaper world, writers create stories to *inform* people as much as possible. In the online business world, we focus more on *persuasive* storytelling. The difference is that you lead them to your point of view. That's the goal of your storytelling.

Know, Like, and Trust

The elements described in Chapter 3 of "Know," "Like," and "Trust" are the central points of every online interaction and every in-person interaction. They are the basis of creating relationships that pay you for a long time.

The key to having people know, like, and trust you is being able to walk them through a process where they absolutely relate to you. They relate to you because you empathize with them, which is one of the key factors in persuasive storytelling.

You have to get people to understand that you know what their situation is. You know where they are and what they have been through. This applies to legal work as much as to any other situation. You're converting them to a point of view.

Attorneys are familiar with this approach. It's what they do when they are speaking to mediators to try to settle a case or making an opening statement in a trial. They tell the story and also help the jury know and like the plaintiff or defendant (whomever they represent).

A trial can go wrong when the jury develops a strong antipathy towards one of the characters. Sometimes that's the plaintiff, and sometimes it's one of the attorneys who is behaving in a way that ticks off the jury. The way people react, perhaps in unpredictable ways, can be like throwing a stick of dynamite into a field and watching what happens. That can be a really important factor in connecting with or turning off the jury.

Approaching Potential Clients

Establishing rapport is also an important factor in connecting with perspective clients. Legal nurse consultants are always looking for the next gig. Be engaging as you communicate the know, like, and trust factors through your stories or any distinctive content about yourself. You have to stand out from the crowd. People have to relate to you and what you have been through. You can do that by using different forms of content:

- Blogs

- Reports

- Videos

These media aren't used nearly enough by legal nurse consultants, and they're good ways to set you apart.

If you're trying to sell yourself online or in the real world, you're in a competitive market. You need to have an advantage to be distinctive, and the authority. Using your own content and your own stories is probably the first strategy.

Content Marketing

Content marketing is an essential step toward branding yourself as an expert. You may take it as a given that you're an expert, but you have to set yourself apart as the expert to whom people want to come.

In a general sense, you have to convince people that you can listen to them, jointly come up with a solution, and try to make it appear that it's their solution. Let them tell you what the problems are. Probe for the solution. Put the solution in front of them. If you've done this well, they'll say, "Oh yeah, that's it. I had a great idea." It becomes their idea.

Then you can collaborate and do whatever it takes to build the case or the action, whatever the situation calls for. The initial interaction makes people feel like you are the person to whom they need to talk and that you are the expert. When you ask probing questions, they give you real answers. The key is to always talk about their situation and their problems so that you can cooperatively get to a solution.

When you're doing content marketing, you're doing kind of the same thing. Make sure you know what the problems are for your marketplace. Then write or create videos or audio about those problems. You empathize with the problems, and then you offer the solution. The solution is either you or a product that you have. It's couched as, "Here's the solution, and where are you going to get that solution? Oh by the way, I have that solution."

Content marketing is a way to write, video, blog, do audios, and build special reports that always point to us as the expert without using braggadocio to do it, without being off-putting about it.

See how different this approach is from the one where website content says "Hire me! Hire me! Hire me! This is what I can do. Hire me! Hire me! Hire me!"

Get Someone Else to Tell Your Story

You can tell me a story about what you've done for somebody else. The only thing better than that is *somebody else* telling others your story. It becomes a lot more authentic. It has a lot more authority than if it comes only from you.

As soon as an attorney says to another attorney, "You ought to use this legal nurse consultant because I've had great results with her," that automatically makes it easier for you to follow through with the referral and get the work. That little barrier of "I don't know you, and I'm not sure if I want to trust my case to you" disappears when you have a referral.

Make sure that if somebody is giving you a referral, they're telling a story about you. You can coach them on telling a story about you if you need to do that. If somebody says, "I love working with Pat because Pat is so sweet," and that's all they're going to say, that's not a very powerful testimonial or referral.

If they say, "I love working with Pat because when we were involved in this case, she looked at it from this perspective. Everybody else missed that, and it was really being able to see the whole picture that helped us go back and win," you get much more detail. The person has to paint the picture about the successful results. See examples of attorney testimonials on this page: http://lncacademy.com/about-pat-iyer/

My Story

A single meeting with an attorney changed my life. I delivered a prize that he won at a drawing. He said, "While you're here, Pat could you look at this case for me?" It involved a neonate who received an overdose of potassium chloride. It was given directly into the neonate's IV port of his catheter.

I said, "Nurses are not allowed to give IV push potassium chloride to patients. It has to be diluted in an IV bag."

"How do you know that?"

"Because I was a staff development instructor and I taught nurses which drugs they could give IV and which ones they had to dilute."

"All the doctors who looked at this case missed that point," he replied.

"That's why you need me." That began a 20-year relationship just on the basis of that first "aha" that he got in talking to me. This first meeting and my discovery led to a long and profitable relationship with the attorney and others in his firm.

It turned out that no, the nurses were not allowed to give IV push potassium chloride. That was a factor in the case the doctors didn't see because they weren't thinking along those lines, and that wasn't their experience.

Analyzing the Story

This story has multiple layers. The setup is that I walked into the office for a completely different reason. I went in to talk to an attorney, but it wasn't really about getting work. That hook gets a listener's or reader's attention. Now the listener is interested in knowing how that's going to work out. It establishes curiosity and promises engaged listening.

Then the attorney asked questions about a case. I factually established my expertise as an instructor who taught nurses which drugs could be given intravenously and which couldn't. An attorney would see how valuable this knowledge is. This takes the listener back to the larger story that he was impressed enough to want to work with me.

The listener is also eager to hear the payoff, which is a good one. The punch line of the story is that a 20-year relationship resulted from that encounter.

That's a big payoff; listeners realize they can go in and not sell themselves so much but answer a question to be of service. That connection is sometimes called a tieback. You go from the end back to the beginning, and you wrap the entire story up that way.

Breaking Down the Steps

The Hook. This is the attention getter.

- "Why am I listening to you now?"

Invite their curiosity. Describe an amazing, shocking, scary, or an interesting moment. People identify with you because of how you begin the story. That has to be the piece that gets the attention. Sometimes it can be a headline, a subhead, or the first couple of sentences of a paragraph, but it has to be very fast. You may have a little leeway face-to-face, but in the online world, people will click away.

The Setup. Go into this once you have their attention. I did this by describing why I was in the attorney's office, to deliver a prize.

The Parachute. Here's where you jump right into the action. For me, the action shifted when he said, "Hey Pat, would you take a look at this case?"

The Theme. This is what the story is about, in this case the issue of the overdose of potassium chloride.

The Transition. This usually occurs in a selling or persuasive situation. The transition comes back to a cliffhanger or a hopeful situation. Is there any hope at this point?

In my transition, I went against the grain. As the educating nurse, I went against all of the doctors in this case who missed this point when I pointed out that the procedure was incorrect.

The Solution. "What's the sale?" The sale provides the solution to the problem that was displayed earlier, the potassium chloride overdose. I didn't have to say anything because he sold it for me. He said, "You're the only one that caught this. Everybody else missed this." The natural response to that was, "That's why you should use me." It was an easy sale at that point.

The Tieback. It's after the sale. The sale is really the persuasive point. It's getting them to take action. The tieback is kind of a reinforcement because it goes all the way back to the beginning. In the beginning, I explained the situation. In the tieback I said that because I walked in with that situation, I ended up having a 20-year relationship with this attorney.

Each step builds on the earlier one to make a well-integrated story. This process works very well in the written world. Craft blog posts and videos using these seven steps.

Ask a Lot of Questions

Asking a lot of questions is the first thing to do because you want to find out what people want to know about. One of the things that never works is trying to convince people.

Make sure that your message matches your audience. If I'm talking to an audience of firefighters about the legal nurse business, they will not be interested unless they have a direct connection somehow to an incident. If I were talking to firefighters about the latest equipment that they needed, they'd be listening. Ask questions about what your audience wants to know.

Determine the content to share with your audience, and then do research. Read the nursing publications, legal publications, and association publications that address major issues. The best way to make yourself an expert is to go figure out what those major issues are and become an expert in those. Do the research and become an expert in those so that you can talk and write about them. You can create podcasts, videos, and special reports about those hot issues.

Be Empathetic

The second part is about empathy. Whenever you're talking to anybody, it's never about *you*. It's always about *them*. It's so hard not to talk about us, but we always want to make sure that we're addressing people's issues. I like to tell people that those are case studies. We're talking about other people and the issues they went through.

In Conclusion

If you are a new LNC and you're trying to get established with content marketing or even established in your business, you can talk about other people, their solutions, and how those things worked. By talking about those other people, you show you know what works even if you haven't done it in the past. You show the kind of empathy and the compassion that you have for that business and those people.

Once again, they need to know you, like you, and they need to be able to trust you. Allow these principles to guide you, and you will be successful.

Key Points

- Stories fill the cases LNCs work on.

- The ability to get people to know like and trust you influences your success as an LNC.

- You have to stand out from the crowd by effectively sharing your content.

- Referrals are more powerful when an attorney gives a specific description of the benefits of using your services.

- Effective stories consist of 7 elements: the hook, setup, parachute, theme, transition, solution, and tieback.

- Determine the content you will share based on asking questions of your target audience and identifying their needs.

CHAPTER 16

How Social Proof Gets You Attorney Clients

Aristotle is the father of these three terms of persuasion: ethos, pathos, and logos. The Greek terms may be unfamiliar to you, but I'll bet you know these concepts by other names. Ethos, pathos, and logos make up some of the most commonly used methods of persuasion. Are you using these concepts in your marketing?

Ethos involves selling yourself. You establish your credibility by detailing your clinical experience, certifications, and client base.

Demonstrate your credibility by sharing your knowledge when you meet with clients to discuss cases or create content for books, articles, and blogs. You use ethos when you stress your character, credibility, or authority. Or you may be on the witness stand and persuasively arguing to make your point.

Use testimonials to establish your credibility. Also, it is helpful when the testimonial comes from a person with authority or good character. In that case, you borrow credibility from other people.

Pathos involves swaying people by emotions. Share stories (closed cases you or others have worked on) and demonstrate how the legal nurse consultant made a difference. You share a poignant story or case and draw out the lessons learned.

Pathos appeals to the emotions. Use a story, an analogy, or something that has some emotion in it that is going to tug at people's heart strings.

Logos involves solid reasoning. Employ statistics, logic, or reasoning to lead the reader to the conclusion you desire.

When you are writing advertising copy, whether it's on your website, in a direct mail piece such as a brochure, or in an email, your main objective is to get the reader to respond in a specific way – buy the product, sign up for the newsletter, volunteer for the event, etc.

Legal nurse consultants who don't use ethos or social proof to gain new customers are overlooking an important marketing technique. Social proof is also referred to as "informational social influence." It is the concept that people will conform to the actions of others under the assumption that those actions are reflective of the correct behavior. There are several ways to demonstrate you have earned social proof.

Video testimonials

Social proof is a big component of sharing information that will reassure your client. Include testimonials on your site and in your marketing materials. Use video testimonials from satisfied clients. The most credible testimonials consist of footage you obtain with a high resolution pocket video camera or an iPhone. Ask the attorney's permission to capture a video testimonial right there. Then load it into the USB port of your computer, upload it to Youtube, copy the embed code, and place it on your website. Make sure the testimonial is brief, to the point, and has good sound. See this example of a testimonial an attorney gave me: http://lnc.tips/attorneytestimonial.

Letters

The second most credible testimonial is in written form, such as a letter or email you received from an attorney who praised your services. You may get an email from an attorney who says, "You did a great job. If it hadn't been for you, I don't know that I would have been able to make it to this figure on this case." Request permission to use this quote. Those testimonials show that someone appreciates your work, and it also makes you a trustworthy individual or company to work with.

Initials and Location

The least credible testimonial does not use a name, or uses a first name only: "LNC, Inc. is a wonderful service. I highly recommend them, AH from Denver, Colorado." The Federal Trade Commission has focused on this type of testimonial and wants to be sure that people using testimonials are able to back up their claims. Those types of testimonials raise a lot of skepticism because people have abused them and have frankly made up those testimonials. Never make up a testimonial.

Always strive to get permission to use the attorney's full name and location.

Getting Testimonials

How do you get testimonials? You ask. Get over your hesitation. I have found that attorneys are quite willing to share testimonials. After you've completed a case or a phase of the case, ask the client to give you a testimonial or fill out a feedback form.

How could you apply this to your legal nurse consulting business? To begin, look through your email inbox and in your snail mail files. Have you ever received a thank-you card or email from a client? You don't have to copy the entire letter. Find a sentence or two that is most compelling. Then copy and paste it into a special file called "social proof" or "testimonials." You probably have more of these comments than you realize.

If you can't find any, simply write to three to five of your best clients, tell them you're developing a new brochure or website, and ask if they would mind saying a few nice words about you. You'd be surprised at how many people are never asked to do so, but (provided you have given great service in the past) would be happy to help you out in this way.

In Conclusion

Use social proof in your emails, on your website or blog, in direct mail pieces, and in other situations in which you are hoping to promote your business. And the good news is that people respond in predictable ways. They will be much more likely to try you out for themselves when they see that others, especially those who they have heard of and/or trust as professionals in their own field, have used and are happy with your services.

I have comments from attorneys about my LNC services on my website at lnc.tips/pattestimonials.

Are you looking for ways to boost your business? Take advantage of an opportunity to speak with me about your business. Complete a few questions at this link: http://lnc.tips/Consult

Key Points

- Ethos, pathos, and logos are three Greek terms of persuasion to use in your marketing.

- Ethos involves selling yourself based on your credibility.

- Pathos involves swaying people on an emotional basis.

- Logos involves using reasoning to be persuasive.

- Use social proof to encourage others to use your services.

- Video testimonials are the most credible kind. Letters are the second most credible testimonials.

- Not supplying the full name and location of an attorney makes a testimonial look suspect.

- Incorporate testimonials in your marketing pieces – brochures, websites, or direct mail pieces.

CHAPTER 17

Story Telling in Marketing

How can you distinguish yourself from the many other LNCs in the field? How do you make yourself unique? How do you express who you are as an individual in a compelling and inviting way? How do you make your brand distinctive and attractive?

Here's a recommendation: Make an emotional connection. Tell a story, as I described in the two previous chapters.

Abandon Stale Phrases and Strategies

Stories capture our attention. We automatically sit up straighter and become more attentive when we hear or read the beginning of a story. The word "content" in comparison sounds a bit duller.

Everyone in marketing and sales talks about content as if it were recently discovered, but content has been around for a long time. Content is subject matter, and you've got to keep on providing it. Good content intrigues attorneys, keeps them interested in you, and makes them want to do business with you. The skills that we have and the results we can produce are all about the outcome.

In Chapter 11, *Rebooting Your Marketing,* we highlighted the importance of identifying your target market. You've read throughout this book about the need to identify your target market of clients and their needs.

The big word now is "persona." What is the persona of your target market? Personas are meant to be living flesh and blood portraits of your target market. Look at your target as a character in a story. The story may be about the determined defense attorney who sifts through a case to look for the defensible aspects. Or your target may be the successful plaintiff attorney who convinces a facility to change their practices as a result of a lawsuit.

What's the turning point in the attorneys' work experiences when they need what you have to offer? That's what you should master. What is the crisis in their lives, their businesses, that leads them to look for you? It could be:

- They are faced with piles of paper and don't have the time to sift through records to capture the details.

- They don't want to get stuck with a non-meritorious case (plaintiff attorneys) or indefensible case (defense attorneys).

- They are not sure if the injuries the plaintiff sustained were due to the motor vehicle accident in question, or a prior one.

When you understand what motivates and concerns your target market, you'll be able to determine the content you should share. You will readily identify your content strategy, which will address their interests, needs, and fears.

Stories Are Part of Your Work

Attorneys who handle cases involving medical issues are confronted every day with multiple opportunities to pull a story out of one of their clients.

If that person is a plaintiff attorney, and she's bringing in a client who was in a car accident and was rear-ended, the story is about what happened to the male driver.

- What was the driver doing right before he was hit from behind?

- How has his life changed as a result of his injury?

- How has his role changed since he had to stop working

- What treatment did he have to go through?

If the attorney is a defense attorney, the story, for example, might be what happened in the operating room. The defense attorney is defending the surgeon.

- What events transpired right before that artery was severed and the blood pressure started dropping?

- What did the surgeon do as a result of that situation?

Attorneys are very much focused on forming stories and thinking of what they do in the framework of a story. You provide a valuable service of helping the attorney develop the story of the case. You suggest questions for depositions, documents to request during discovery, and ideas for the case theory.

LNCs have very dramatic material to work with. Most professional service marketers or professional service consultants are not dealing with life and death. When you talk about cutting an artery, or people injured in an auto accident, these are ultimately life and death issues or severe injury and consequences that could go on for the rest of somebody's life.

Medical cases have perfect storytelling material because there's a lot at stake. A story is defined by conflict. There has to be some obstacle, something that has to be overcome to reach the outcome.

In Chapter 15, *Content Marketing with Stories*, I shared a model of telling a story that included 7 elements: the hook, setup, parachute, theme, transition, solution, and tieback.

Here's another framework for putting together a story: the "abccds" of a story.

"A" = Action

The best stories start with an action. For example, start at that traumatic moment where the mistake occurred.

You are speaking over the phone to an attorney who is looking for an expert witness. Her description of the story reminds you of another one related to the same type of injury. You say, "I worked on a case like that; may I tell you about it?"

"Sure, I'd like to hear about it."

"The anesthesiologist noticed the patient's blood pressure was rapidly dropping, and her pulse rate increased. The surgeon couldn't suction out the blood fast enough. He'd cut the vena cava. The patient was in deep trouble, and the situation had to be corrected immediately."

Suddenly we have a dramatic situation. "Instead of doing the right thing, the doctor complicated the situation by doing the wrong thing."

"What happened?" the attorney asks. You've created suspense.

Consultants often think they need to have the answers all the time. What you want to do is set up suspense. You set up a story in action. Imagine the best movies you've ever seen. Don't they usually start in action? Play the movie. Let people see it.

"B" = Back Story

You always want to get people eager to hear the story before you take this step backwards.

"What's the back story?"

"How did she get into this situation?"

"Carla had a horrible automobile accident. She was rushed into the emergency room. There was no time to do a complete set of diagnostic tests. The emergency team had to make some judgments about which were her most critical injuries."

You don't want to get too deep into the back story because the back story might actually become the story. Keep the story moving forward. Be clear about what your ending is going to be so that your back story is building towards that.

"C" = Conflict

There's got to be some kind of conflict, something at stake.

What do you get if you win? What do you get if you lose? What do you *not* get if you lose? There always has to be something at stake.

"C" = Crisis

There has to be a turning point. That final turning point in any story is the climax.

"The patient died, the patient became a paraplegic, or the patient was restored to health because this doctor did the right thing."

"D" = Destination

The destination is the final turning point. What happens to the patient's life after an incident? Does she worsen and then die? Does she survive with permanent injuries? Does she fully recover?

Thinks ABCCD (Action, Back Story, Conflict, Crisis, Climax, Destination) or even "Where do we go from here?"

- Here are the lessons learned.
- Here's what we have to fix for the next time.

If you just keep ABCCD in your head, you can tell a good story. It's a good, simple formula.

The Hero's Journey

The Hero's Journey is the classic quest story. You've seen this played out in countless books and movies. The movie starts by introducing a character. You develop an affection for the character and learn more about the person. Then comes a sudden crisis or a conflict. The person gets in trouble, and then the trouble has to get resolved. That's the final destination. Why do we read journalism? Why do we read stories? Stories start somewhere that's engaging. Think of how a great novel pulls you in right from the beginning. You are intrigued. You want to know what happens next.

Consider how a plaintiff attorney uses a story in the opening statement. She creates a character for the jury. She shows pictures of the patient, his family, his interests, and his life. The attorney paints a picture of the kind of person he was before he fell into a vat of acid at his work site. Then she describes the incident and the aftermath and tells the jury she will prove the employer was negligent in not enforcing safety practices.

Expert Witnesses Use Stories

Suppose you are an expert witness. You can weave a story into your testimony. Your analogies and illustrations help the jury understand. If you can find an opening, it can be very powerful to tell people an engaging story that's structured in a way that keeps them a little bit breathless wanting to know what happened. The payoff has to be in the direction you want it to be. Let the jurors see the picture.

Think of expert witnesses giving opinions about whether the incident that occurred in the healthcare facility was the result of negligence. They have to be able to convey their opinions and use analogies and examples the jury would understand.

Whenever you're telling a story, tell it with the end in mind. Everything should build towards that ending. The Hero's Journey guides you to construct your story backwards so that it ends up exactly where you want it to end up; you don't meander. A lot of people meander, and then they take all the power out of their story by rambling. You've seen that happen, I bet.

Come to a dramatic point. There should be a phrase at the end that's usually some kind of payoff phrase. It comes out of the details of the story. It helps people remember the story. In Chapter 15, *Content Marketing with Stories*, I called this the tieback – it brings the listener full circle to the beginning of the story.

Weave stories into your marketing. Include them in blogs and videos. You'll keep your reader or viewer's attention and be able to show your expertise.

Promised Customer Experience

Part of the story of your company is how you handle clients. A lot of professional service people, consultants, and experts think if they say what they do, that's enough to get them hired.

At the heart of marketing is making a promise or making some kind of offer.

- This is what we do.

- This is what you'll get.

But that's not enough; that's just talking *at* your potential client. What's wrong with that marketing approach? That's going to get you very little business. It may get you some, especially if you have a reputation and people know you, but a brand or your business proposition is bigger than that. It's more than *what* you do. It's about what your customers *get*. Your attorney clients care about what they receive from you. How do you make their practice easier?

There are thousands of legal nurse consultants who want to provide services to attorneys. What differentiates you?

Your brand makes a *promise* of an experience. That's only 50% of the equation. The other half is the client's *experience* of that promise to deliver. What's that like? It's bigger than features and benefits of what you have to offer. It's the experience that they have from working with you. I'm sure at some point in your life you bought a product or service because of what it promised to do for you. Then you were disappointed in what you got – an average product but lousy customer service. Don't disappoint your clients by giving them lousy customer service.

Story Tools

Story tools help people get out of the usual marketing language of enumerating a generic list of LNC services. They start to suggest the experience that your customer can have in working with you. As you begin to tell stories and case histories, attorneys think, "That's the kind of person I want to work with."

Story tools are more than a left brain list of skills and attributes. It's also the use of right brain creativity pulling in emotional and psychological dimensions. Your prospect picks up on these dimensions and concludes, "You're the kind of person I want to be around. You're the kind of person who's got the right feel."

A brand is the promise of an experience and your client's experience of that promise. Once you have delivered your services, get feedback. Ask your clients:

- "How was this?"
- "How was it working with me?"

Get feedback deeper than that you delivered the results. Knowing how your clients perceived the experience of working with you is very powerful, especially in the business-to-business arena. Most business owners don't go that far. They think if they say, "We do this," that it's enough, but it's not. You have to be able to explain to a prospect, "Why should you want to work with me?"

I found that when attorneys asked me for an expert witness, I could close the sale more readily by saying, "Let me refer you to Nurse _____. I have gotten great feedback that she testifies well." Your clients want to know how others experienced your services.

Legal Nurse Consulting Marketing Materials

Consider these steps when designing your legal nurse consulting marketing materials:

1.   Outline the problem the attorney is dealing with.
2.   Describe both the current situation and the ideal situation.
3.   Show how the current situation could be improved.
4.   Outline how your services create the ideal situation.
5.   Show how using your services will solve the problem.

Example:

Look at how this copy addresses the attorney's problem.

You are a plaintiff medical malpractice attorney handling lots of potential claims. You don't know which ones have merit. That person who just left your office wants an answer and fast. She left a stack of medical records with you. You know you should attempt to go through them, but you aren't sure what you should be looking for, and who can make sense of electronic medical records, anyway? Before you invest thousands into this case, you really need to know what this case is about. Was it just a bad outcome?

You think, "If I just had a medical professional to ask to look at this case, I'd feel much more comfortable about taking it." You'd feel assured that you had a case worth investigating. You'd know what to tell the client when she calls to find out if you are going to take her case.

As a legal nurse consultant, I help plaintiff attorneys determine which cases have merit. I assist you in weeding out the non-meritorious cases.

When you give me those medical records, I can pinpoint the issue faster and at a lower cost than having an expert witness be the first medical professional to review the case. That way you can spend your precious resources on cases with merit. And free up your desk space.

Call me today at 888-888-8888 for help with your medical malpractice cases.

Make sense? No, don't copy this and put it on your website. Use this example as a way to stimulate your thinking about how your legal nurse consulting services help attorneys. Look at your marketing materials and your website. Are you talking to your prospect about his problems or just about yourself?

Many legal nurse consultants send marketing letters to attorneys. Here is a typical letter:

Dear _____,

We would like to thank you for your ongoing confidence in our services. We appreciate your business and look forward to continuing our relationship with you.

How can we help you now? Do you have cases that you would love to move forward and clear off your desk? We would be happy to help make that happen! We can organize and summarize the records for you, identify missing records, and locate experts. We can also develop detailed chronologies and timelines and perform literature searches. If complex medical procedures and terminology are slowing you down, let us help with clear explanations and exhibits.

We enjoy working with you and anticipate the opportunity to assist you soon on future cases.

Enjoy your day!

This letter is not bad, but it could be improved upon. If you look at the sentence structure, you see a lot of sentences start with "We." Here is the issue. Your client or prospect cares far more about his or her immediate needs and the benefits obtained from your services than about what you have to offer. By making a simple revision, your marketing letter will speak to the client's needs and the benefits you provide.

Don't assume that the person reading the letter will understand the benefits. The revision below spells them out in more detail. The formula is "lead with benefits, follow with services." Start the letter focusing on benefits and then add details of services.

Dear _____,

We would like to thank you for your ongoing confidence in our services. We appreciate your business and look forward to continuing our relationship with you.

How can we help you now? Do you have cases that you need to move forward and clear off your desk? We would be happy to help make that happen!

- Do you need medical records organized and summarized so you can get a clear picture of the plaintiff's injuries and quickly locate information?

- Do you need to know what records are missing so that you won't be caught by surprise?

- Do you have a case with a plaintiff who was in more than one accident and you have to know which injuries relate to the accident you are defending?

- Do you have a case that needs a well-qualified expert witness?

- Do you need detailed chronologies and timelines or literature searches so you have a clearer understanding of the details and type of care rendered?

If complex medical procedures and terminology are slowing you down, let us help with clear explanations and exhibits. We enjoy working with you and anticipate the opportunity to assist you soon on future cases.

Best wishes,

The key point here is to think about the needs of your client. Keep that foremost in your thoughts when you are communicating, via your website or a personal letter, to your client.

Compelling Subject Lines

I've pointed out how valuable it is to offer something of value in order to build a list of prospects – attorneys who need your services. You give them something: a white paper, a video, or whatever it is. Invite them to fill out a form, and then you get their email address. Once you've delivered the free material, send periodic emails to your list to provide them valuable information and to stay top of mind. (I cover writing opt-in material in in one of my courses, *How to Create an Irresistible Opt In Offer.* See the details at this link. **http://lnc.tips/CreateOptins**

How do you get the attorney to open your email? You want to get your target's interest. They have a problem. They have a big, pervasive problem. You want to flag that problem because then they say, "You get me. You understand the situation that I'm in." Then what you have to offer to solve this category, this target's big, pervasive problem.

It just so happens what you have to offer is the ultimate solution to that problem. You want them to say, "How do you do that?" You've gotten their attention, and then you can tell stories. For example, "We worked on a case involving an anesthesiologist who hung IV bags on a sterilizer in order to warm them, but did not check the temperature before infusing them into the patient's vein." You give a story that gets your prospect engaged, and then you have some kind of call to action.

Conclude with "If you're facing a similar situation, or you have a knotty problem that you just can't cut through, talk to us."

The attorney has a problem. You have the ultimate solution to that problem. Answer the question of how you arrived at that solution. Give them case studies to prove it, but between those two steps you might also talk about the cost of *not* fixing the problem.

You say, "Here we have a process. Here's how we work. Here are some success stories to prove it. End with a call to action. That's the total selling logic of any marketing piece whether it's big or small that you should be following. It's a very effective outline.

The headline should somehow flag the prospects. It can be a question. It can be a startling fact. It can start with "How" or "Why" or a number. For some crazy reason, odd numbers are more powerful than even numbers. Rather than "The 6 Mistakes You Should Avoid," it's "The 7 Mistakes You Should Avoid in Handling a Labor and Delivery Case." That's more powerful than "6." I can't explain it. I've seen it work. Using the word, "mistakes" is sometimes more powerful than the word, "solutions" alone because everybody wants to avoid mistakes, especially in the legal world.

Start with a "How" or a "Why" or a dramatic statement and say, "Is this you?" "Are you in need of a difficult-to-locate expert witness? Call us. We can help." The attorney says, "I need that. I want that." Then talk about what you do. Prove it with a success story and say, "If you want to talk some more, I promise you that the first conversation we have will give you valuable answers, and then we can decide whether there's a fit."

This is a logical expression of the outline I showed before: the problem and the ultimate solution.

One of the biggest problems that attorneys face is that they have a pile of medical records that they need to understand, and they don't have time to go through them. They don't understand all of the medical terms. They don't have the patience to set aside seven or eight hours to read every part of the record that's germane. A legal nurse consultant can help them with that pain point.

Translated into an opening for sales piece, this might read:

"Is this you? You've got a stack of medical reports. The terminology is complete gobbledy-gook to you. There are procedures you don't understand. You don't have the seven or eight hours to plow through it all. You need a guiding hand."

You could further refine this into bullet points. The main point is to fully describe their big, pervasive problem. They're completely overwhelmed by all this documentation that they can't even begin to understand or deal with. They need somebody to take them by the hand, lead them out of the woods, and find the big thread in all those files that will crack the case.

In Conclusion

The more you can show that you understand and empathize with attorneys, and the more fully you demonstrate that you can come up with a happy ending, the more work you'll have.

Key Points

- Make your brand distinctive by weaving in stories to your marketing materials. We are conditioned to enjoy stories.

- Be exquisitely aware of the problems your clients face so you can determine the content you should share and the services you will provide.

- Use a storytelling model consisting of action, back story, conflict, crisis, and destination.

- The Hero's Journey is a frequently used model for telling a story.

- Expert witnesses should weave stories into their testimony when possible.

- Make sure you deliver the quality you promise. Ask your clients for feedback about how they experienced your services.

- Review your competition's websites. Many of them say the same thing. Make yours stand out by addressing the attorney's problem rather than providing the same bland list of services.

- Use compelling subject lines and stories in emails to grab and hold attention.

SECTION 4

Marketing with Exhibiting

CHAPTER 18

Building a Solid Foundation for Exhibiting

If your marketing efforts get people engaged, you've built relationships, and you've provided a memorable experience for your prospects, what do you have? You've got influence, more revenue, and confidence. This is what being an entrepreneur is all about.

One way to build an LNC practice is to create a powerful presence at a conference or a convention. You can show up and network your way through an event, or you can show up, take a piece of the real estate, i.e., exhibit, and then create your presence in that space.

The Return on Investment from Trade Shows

Picture yourself making a cold call on an attorney. The receptionist announced your presence to an attorney, who has agreed to see you in his office for a few minutes. You're sitting on the other side of his desk. You see this: He's sitting with his arms across his chest, his legs crossed, and a frown on his face. He's asking himself, "Who is this person? Why should I spend my time talking with this vendor?" You describe the benefits of your services and he says, "I'd like to think about it."

You make a follow-up call, and he comes to the phone. He is still gruff. He conveys to you, "Oh, you again. You got by my minions again. What is it you wanted to sell me?"

You speak to him a third time. He says, "All right. Let's get down to business."

Those first two interactions are eliminated when you exhibit at a trade show. You are meeting the decision makers face to face.

Three elements will make your conference/convention experience more powerful.

1. Identify the right conferences to go to.

2. Understand what your goal is by either attending or exhibiting at that conference.

3. Carefully prepare your booth and giveaways.

How to Choose the Conference

When I was running my legal nurse consulting business, I flew to San Francisco with another staff member and exhibited at a conference called "RIMS." I thought that there would be lots of attorneys there involved in the defense side, but it attracted lots of insurance people and a few risk managers. It was a huge expense, and it yielded zero results.

I realized I would have been far better off finding out who was in the audience before I bought a table, shipped all of my supplies, and then watched people walk by saying, "Legal nurse consultants? I'm not sure what you do and why I need you, but I'm going to go over here to grab these premiums from this table because I come here every year. They disappear rapidly and I want to get mine."

Be crystal clear on who's in the audience before you make a commitment. I made an expensive error.

Choosing Your Show

Choosing a trade show may depend both on your area of expertise and how easy it is for you to get to the show. It's important to be aware that every trade show is local, whether it's been billed as a local, regional, national, or international event. Seventy percent of every trade show's attendees are coming from a 300-mile radius.

Let's say your LNC business requires you to be eye-ball-to-eyeball with your client. You're located in New Jersey and thinking about going to a show in Chicago. Unless you are prepared to make numerous trips to Chicago, avoid that show. Instead, you go to a show in Philadelphia or New York City.

Obviously, if you live in higher populated areas, you can have a larger audience from a shorter distance. If you're going to the show simply because it's the national show of that industry, but you're not geographically prepared to service that city, don't go.

Choose Your Kind of Participation

Probably the ideal conference is a place where the attorneys are coming to be exposed to what's new and different in the marketplace. They are looking for what's going on that will help their business.

Attorneys may be coming to get CLE (Continuing Legal Education) if they have to renew their license on a periodic basis.

If attorneys are only one part of the group who are coming, you might be better off as an attendee rather than an exhibitor. Knowing the exact purpose of the conference is a good place to start.

In addition, when you're an attendee, you have an opportunity to network more freely. You get a chance to listen to sessions to determine the challenges and struggles attorneys face.

If you're exhibiting, you are more rooted to the exhibit space. You're waiting for people to come to you, and you're listening for key words.

Another option is to sponsor an attorney event. If you live in a smaller town and you're working with local attorneys, you could sponsor one of their lunches or meetings. In exchange, you are often offered five minutes or ten minutes of dedicated time before them.

Beware the desire to accomplish your goals in the quickest way possible. Stay focused on which events are best for you. It could be very expensive to invest in exhibit space and conference attendance; choose wisely.

Carefully Prepare Your Booth and Giveaways

Make sure your space clearly identifies who you are.

I'm a huge fan of the lightweight retractable 6 ft. banners that allow you to highlight some of the key things about what you do, why you do them, and who you do them for.

Signage is important whether you're going to use a banner that goes across your back of the booth or you're going to create one of those retractable stands. It's certainly worth the investment, especially if you plan on using exhibits as a lead generation tool.

Your space should have height, texture, and color. You can tie into the theme of the event or season. Highlight your brand. That's the most important element.

What goes on your signs or banners is critical. You're going to miss a lot of your potential audience when you use the traditional header copy of:

- WE'RE THE ABC COMPANY – Your Legal Nurse Consultant

- THIS IS XYZ, Inc. – #1 Since _____

- 123 ENTERPRIZE – The Solution To YOUR Problems

Attorneys are unwilling to wait around to ask, "In what industry do you lead?" "In what line are you #1?" "Which of my problems can you solve?" Knowing how to grab an attorney's attention is essential for a successful trade show experience.

One pitfall that exhibitors encounter is relying on the name of their business to provide information. "Jennifer Green Associates" says nothing. "Your Source for Expert Legal Nurse Consulting" is extremely specific. People who are involved in this area will stop in the aisle and say, "You do that?"

They don't care about the name of your company. They want to know what's in it for them. While you're proud of your company's name, if it doesn't tell people what you do, come up with a different heading.

Grab an Attorney's Attention When You Tell Him What You Do as a Legal Nurse Consultant

When you design the wording for your banner stand or display unit, a major key component is for you to tell your audience (attorney attendees) WHAT YOU DO in your lead copy. It's like a newspaper or internet article headline – it's the first thing attorneys read, and when it fails to grab their attention and stop them in their tracks, it may actually cost you a major prospect.

Gone are the days of simply proclaiming WHO YOU ARE – in today's super-saturated marketplace, attorneys are selfish with their time and need to be told quickly and simply, "Here's What's In It For YOU!" And that has to happen in your header and initial body copy.

Don't Make Attorneys Guess at Your Legal Nurse Consulting Services

How many times have YOU walked through a trade show, seen a booth that catches your eye and then tried to figure out what they do/sell, who they serve and yes, what's in it for YOU? When you're unable to quickly determine this information from reading their copy, you simply move on – perhaps passing up a valuable tool, process, or solution to YOUR problem that's simply poorly articulated by the exhibitor.

Attorneys will stop to talk to you if they have the problems that your copy addresses. How do you grab an attorney's attention? Be clear in stating:

"Here's What We Do For YOU"

"How Are YOU Handling THIS?"

Use an Attention-Getting Display to Attract Attorney Clients

The first time I exhibited, I put a three-ring binder on the panel of my booth with a sign that said, "How Much Medical Malpractice is in This Medical Record?" It was unsophisticated but effective in getting medical malpractice attorneys to stop.

Those who deal with or have problems with THIS are going to stop, visit, or at least pick up your product/service/solution information sheet.

When you grab attorneys' attention, successfully solve their problem, meet their need, and answer their question in your header and back wall copy, you're way ahead of your competition and far more likely to get attorneys stopping to talk to you.

What Should You Give Away?

What do we do about attracting people to our booth? Make it engaging for them. Instead of having a promotional item for everybody, you might decide to use a spinning wheel. Allow people to spin a wheel to figure out what they get. You might provide a fishbowl with a drawing for something of value that maybe is a little bit higher end.

The other items you give away can be pens, notepads, or a calendar if it's the beginning of the year. What can you select to reflect your specialty? Deciding what you're going to give away at a booth is a matter of your goals, the type of attendees, and your budget.

Besides giving out things, be sure to give business cards and have something that you can do to follow up after the event. People who go through a conference like to find one or two memorable things that they're going to follow up with afterwards. The question you need to ask yourself is, "What's going to be memorable for you?" That sometimes requires an earlier conversation about how you want to show up as a brand.

Be wary of people with big bags walking down the aisles and scooping things off the table and into their bags two, three, four, and five at a time. Not everybody does this, but the ones who do it stand out.

After a while you start recognizing them when they have made their second or third circuit through the room. You see them coming, and you put your premiums under the table. "You've taken enough." Your goal is to get the premiums in the hands of people who can give you business.

Selective Gift Giving

Use promotional items to:

- Help you define your brand
- Reinforce the solution you provide to the market
- Thank your clients and as an ongoing relationship builder

Pens are a great giveaway. You make that a Tier 1 (lowest value) item; then you might give away the Tier 2 items when somebody actually has a conversation with you. They might get something "better" or more valuable. The Tier 3 might be something that they get after they have worked with you.

I've used that method in my own legal nurse consulting business of having some items on the table that are inexpensive. Some are more expensive. Ensure the people who are reaching for the more expensive items have given you a business card so that you can stay in touch or continue to market to that person.

In one type of giveaway that I created, I had informational cards with medical definitions or medical terms in a little binder. My staff sent periodic new cards as supplements to the binder. Attorneys absolutely loved them. They went wild over them even though it was information that they could get from Google. They were nicely presented, printed, designed, and cute looking. It was also easier for them to put these cards in a desk drawer and pull them out as they needed than having to do searches on a computer.

Promotional items don't have to be expensive to be valuable. It's important to understand that. Always give away something that has your name and your contact information, whether it's an email or a phone number. I'm a fan of both. If you're going to spend money on giveaways, you need to provide a way for prospects to reach you.

Giveaways for Follow-Up

After a conference is over, you may use promotional items for the follow-up. Instead of email follow-up, consider sending a series of little boxes. They have something in them that reinforces your brand or the message that you're trying to show these attorneys. It makes you different from everybody else.

A phrase, "lumpy mail," refers to any type of dimensional direct mail that you're mailing. You might build on this aspect of contact by sending out a series of at least three items. The giveaways should be clever without being confusing.

I'm a fan of simple.

Market with Creativity

Marketing provides you with an opportunity to test your creativity, knowing that some things will work better than others. Step out of your comfort zone a little even if it may sound hokey to you. You are using the right side of your brain when you are creative, whereas much of nursing is left-brain reliant. Nursing practice is succinct and involves direct steps. To be a good marketer, you have to erase all of that and just start scribbling.

If you identify your goals and explore what makes you unique, you'll identify your brand message. This will make it easier to select promotional items, marketing materials, and marketing messaging. Be a little creative and playful in the marketing process.

An earlier book in this series, **Creating a Successful Legal Nurse Consulting Practice**, offers two additional chapters on exhibiting. *Legal Nurse Consultant Marketing* is available at this link: **http://lnc.tips/creatingseries**

How to Put Your Best Professional Foot Forward

How you dress at a booth will reflect on you. Attorneys expect LNCs to be professional, credible and expert. Your dress is going to rule you in or count you out pretty quickly. I once exhibited next to a couple of blonde ladies who exposed more flesh in their outfit then I think I have ever seen at a professional exhibit. They were hired specifically by the attorney who offered demonstrative evidence in computer simulations. The women were well developed, had beautiful legs, and had long blonde hair.

I watched how men reacted to them when these women were in a booth next to mine. Men coming from opposite directions had a head-on collision because they were not looking ahead. They were looking at the ladies. The chef and the entire kitchen staff came out to stare at the women.

I don't know if this attorney got any really good leads, but the women stirred up a whole lot of attention. One of my clients said it best. While we were talking, my back was to the girls. When he spotted them, I saw his eyes get really wide, and he said, "Who are the bathing beauties?"

I do not recommend this approach to attract clients.

Your Interactions with Potential Clients are Crucial

Attorneys want to work with business owners they can do business with. It brings up one final point, which is if you are exhibiting, you need to show up at the booth. It's very difficult to farm out that responsibility to somebody else.

It is helpful to have someone else in your booth who understands the goals of exhibiting, your company's services and competitive advantage, and how to interact with prospects and clients. Your helper should be an engaging and outgoing person.

My book, *How to Manage Your LNC Business and Clients: Top Tips for Success* includes a chapter devoted to mastering business communication. There are 6 chapters specifically on deepening client relationships. Order it at **http:// lnc.tips/Creating series**.

In Conclusion

Participating in conferences is a strategy that I found to be very successful in building my legal nurse consulting business, but it's also a long-term one. I think we all go to the exhibits wanting instant gratification, to come away with a huge stack of qualified prospects. Sometimes your success in exhibiting is marked by a slow process of attorneys seeing you over and over again, getting to know you, feeling comfortable with you, and talking with you. Exhibiting is a technique that can be very effective in establishing those relationships.

Where people get a little bit confused is not understanding that marketing is all about getting a prospect to become a customer. There's actually a continuum in that process. Marketing is all about getting the prospect to make their own decision to choose you.

Key Points

- It is much faster to meet and engage an attorney prospect at a trade show than it is to make cold calls.

- Choose to exhibit at an attorney conference based on location, match for your services and your budget.

- Every trade show is heavily attended by people who live within a 300-mile radius.

- You have the choice of attending a show to network or to be on the exhibit floor. Either method will give you an opportunity to meet attorneys.

- Lightweight retractable banner stands are convenient and versatile.

- Your booth signs should clearly state how you help attorneys.

- Any giveaway you select should have room for your contact information.

- Send giveaways in follow up mailings after the trade show.

- Unleash your creativity to think of unique ways to select promotional items and marketing materials.

- Dress appropriately for the setting.

- Recognize that exhibiting may not yield instant results but is a long-term strategy that builds relationships.

CHAPTER 19

Creating a Successful Exhibiting Experience

I can attribute a lot of the growth of my legal nurse consulting business to my experiences exhibiting at attorney trade shows. This is not only because I've learned the best practices for the trade show floor or the attorney conference floor. What happens before as well as after the show is equally important.

In general, a legal nurse consultant should become involved in exhibiting when he or she has focused attention on two or three key areas of expertise. You may think you want to go and be everything to everybody. In fact, the attorneys who are at the shows are looking for the specifics of how you can help them with cases.

You may want to work with lawyers who specialize in a certain type of case, such as medical malpractice or personal injury. You can focus on one or two. The more specific you can be, the more effective a trade show will be.

Focus on Key Services

Focus is of primary importance. Instead of marketing a long list of services, design your signs and discussions around the most frequently requested services.

Eighty percent of your business comes from 20% of your customer base, so identify the two or three products or services you offer that are your highest money makers.

Lead with your strengths, the skills that you can talk most professionally about with the greatest amount of detail. Don't overlook the power of name dropping.

- "I've worked closely with Mr. Prominent Plaintiff Attorney on his cases" or

- "I was on the staff of ABC Hospital and we actually wrote the rules for this particular procedure for the Baylor College of Medicine."

Identify and focus on your key two or three areas of expertise.

Interpersonal Skills

It is critical to show up a certain way at a trade show. Don't sit behind your booth. Be in front or alongside your booth so that you feel a part of the action versus forcing people to come into your space. Your position in the booth will make you more welcoming and inviting versus more closed off and isolated.

Extroverts typically enjoy the opportunity to meet potential clients and existing clients who attend a trade show. Introverts may find the environment to be more stressful and need to give themselves periodic breaks to regroup. Although I am an introvert, I learned to enjoy trade shows once I found out how to pace myself. Refer to *How to Get More Cases: Sales Secrets for Legal Nurse Consultants* for more tips on how personality influences sales

Ask very specific open-ended questions rather than seeing somebody walking by and saying, "Hi, how are you doing? How is the show going for you? Can I tell you about my company?" By that time they're gone.

Instead, if you focus on personal injury cases, look them straight in the eye and ask, "How are you handling your slip and fall cases?"

If I'm a legal nurse consultant who has expertise, background and knowledge in slip and fall cases, I want to work with a law firm that specializes in that. Ask everybody who walks by,

- "Hi, how do you handle your slip and fall cases?"

- "How does your firm handle your slip and fall cases?"

- "How do you personally handle (whatever the primary expertise that you're looking to represent)?"

You can ask that question to either promote your expertise or to identify the law firm that is handling that kind of case. This is qualifying the prospect. "Is your firm one of those that has this as part of their portfolio?" It's a question that is geared to requiring the person to either qualify or disqualify himself or their firm.

If you specialize in a niche area, the question could be, "Who in your firm handles your operating room cases?" or "Who in your firm handles workers compensation cases?" The more specific you can get, the more likely you are to get the right answer.

It could be, "How do you handle slip and fall cases?" "I don't, but we do handle those in our firm, and you need to talk to Sue Jones or Bill Watson." Now that you have that information, you're able to call Sue Jones or Bill Watson and say, "Henry Smith, your senior attorney, was at the XYZ show and recommended that I give you a call."

If you have your questions prepared, then you can launch into them. You should watch the reactions of the prospect instead of feeling like you have to babble in the hopes of interesting the attorney in your services.

Be specific and hard-hitting. The moment it becomes clear that you and the person stopping at your booth have nothing to give to each other, tell them nicely to have a good show.

The faster you can separate the wheat from the chaff, the more time you have to talk to the wheat. You don't want to miss some of the wheat because you fail to qualify the chaff. They're just there to pass some time, so you ask an open-ended question that figuratively asks, "Are you qualified enough for me to visit with you?"

Be Prepared

People who are doing exhibiting need to prepare, develop a script, use skills to handle visitors, and know how to follow up. Exhibiting is not something that involves walking in, setting up a table, standing back, and thinking that it's all going to flow. It took me quite a few exhibits to understand what I was doing there, how to approach people, and how to respond.

One very important issue is that you don't want to spend a lot of time getting absorbed discussing a case with an attorney. Three, four, five, or ten other people may walk by because they don't want to interrupt you when you're talking to somebody.

A prolonged conversation actually can cost you other opportunities. Suppose at the end of the prolonged conversation the attorney sits there and says, "You know what, I have to think about it. I'm not sure I want to proceed." You think, "Wow, I just gave you 10 minutes, and I lost opportunities to talk to 10 other people."

Instead, say, "I would love to be able to have a more thorough conversation with you, maybe tomorrow. Could we meet at 8:00 for coffee?" or "Are you free for lunch? Could we meet?" Just let them know that their time is important, and you want to be 100% present so that you can hear what they're really looking for. Especially if you're the only person in the booth, be respectful of those people who are walking by.

Gather Information

There are multiple layers in the process of building a strong foundations for exhibiting. It's not about ordering 500 pens. It's about the signage and about the focus of the exhibit. It's about how you can connect with people, work on them, and make sure that when you go back to your office and you have a business card in your hand. You remember what type of cases that attorney worked on.

If the attorney said, "I want you to call me on Monday because I have a case involving a patient who fell in the hospital," then you know that it is John that you need to speak to about that specific case.

Bring a notebook and a pen to your booth or some other method of taking notes. Be very sensitive to the fact that there are going to be people who are trying to transact business if you will. You want to be very firm because you're showing up as a professional. Say, "I want to have time to listen to you about the case so I can answer your questions correctly. Let's schedule a time to talk again after this is over." Don't be afraid to say that. Attorneys understand firmness. They are succinct. They want to do a job and get it done. Be respectful of your own time so that you don't feel overwhelmed with trying to talk to every person. Some people are just going to stop by your booth and pick up one of your giveaways.

Remember that every attorney who walks by your booth is not a good fit for you. If somebody walks by your booth without talking to you, it is not 99.9% of the time you. It's them being very focused on exactly what they're looking for or not needing your services. Accept that it's better to walk away with 50 great business cards of people with whom you can follow-up as opposed to 500 cards from people whom now you have to go through and start marketing to. I know a lot of people will say, "Success is in the numbers," and to a degree they're right. But I would always rather have a smaller number of quality leads than a bigger number of cards from people who are blanks to me.

How to respond to "I already have a legal nurse consultant I work with"

Whether you're speaking to an attorney at your booth, in a meeting during the conference, or in a follow-up situation, you need to be able to answer this question.

If you say, "Oh, I see" and turn your attention to the next person, that's called giving up without an effort. Want to know a better way to respond?

You could begin a dialogue about the other LNC when the attorney says, "I already have a legal nurse consultant." Define the person's role. "Is this person an (in-house) employee?" If the attorney says yes, you could ask whether this person works part time or full time. "Are there times when the LNC is overloaded and could use an independent LNC to help with cases?" I've gotten cases from in-house LNCs who have come to my independent LNC business to locate expert witnesses.

If the attorney says the LNC is an independent LNC, you might say, "I'll be here if you ever want to make a change."

This is a better response, but it is also called giving up without an effort. You might be thinking, "I'm better than her." How do you know? You'll put the attorney on the defensive with this question because it attacks his choice.

Consider asking a question that raises doubt.

When the attorney says, "I already have a legal nurse consultant" you may ask,

- "How did you select her?"

- "How do you ensure you are getting the best services?"

- "How often do you review who you are using as vendors?" (This plants a suggestion that a review is normal.)

As you get more experience asking this question and hear the names of LNCs the attorneys are working with, use questions to get the attorney to doubt his position. Prepare your questions, the attorney's possible answers, and your next questions.

You won't convince everyone to give you a try. But situations change:

- The attorney's practice requires additional support.

- The LNC moves away, retires or closes the business.

- The LNC gets too busy to work on the attorney's cases.

- The attorney knows someone who is looking for an LNC and remembers you.

It's Not Necessarily About Selling

While you don't want to cast an overly wide net, you also don't want to cast one that's too narrow. Some people think that they will magically meet five people with whom they can immediately establish a business relationship. That's not what you're at the conference for, and that's not what people come to the conference for. If you go to the event thinking you're going to immediately sell somebody, you're going to be very disappointed and you're going to make some people awfully mad.

Understand that a trade show or attorney conference is to build relationships, not only business but personal. Have a notepad and take notes when you hear somebody say, "It's Thursday afternoon, and I've got to get home because my 14-year-old son is quarterbacking the football team tomorrow night" or "My daughter is in a recital this weekend."

When you follow up with them, ask, "Hey, Harry, thank you for stopping by the booth. How did your son do at that football game?" or "How successful was your daughter's recital?"

The old adage is, "People don't care what you've got until they know that you care." This is very true. You can exhibit caring by taking notes like that. If you don't take them, you're not going to remember them.

Another way to put this is, "They won't remember who you are, but they will remember how you made them feel."

The underlying temptation you need to avoid is the desire to go to a trade show for instant gratification, to make a sale on the spot. Sometimes that happens. It gladdens the heart of a legal nurse consultant to see one of her clients walk in with a case under his arms saying, "I knew I would see you here, so I wanted to bring you the medical records."

The other myth is that it's wrong to follow up too soon. It is never too soon.

Instead of packing up the booth at the end of the show, get your plane ticket for the following night. Make arrangements to take one good prospect to dinner and the next morning another prospect to breakfast. You'll go by one of their offices during the morning, and you're taking another one to lunch before you take the afternoon flight home.

You make those four or five appointments the day after the show, and you're likely to have a couple of cases to take home. At this point, when you follow up with the other ones, you can say, "Mr. Jones, I appreciate you coming by the booth. I told you that we could get to you in about three weeks, but we've already picked up three new clients, and I want to make sure I can speak with you. When can we meet?"

It puts you in a whole different mindset from the person who comes back with 20 leads on a Thursday night and can't get in touch with them on Friday because there are end-of-week things to do. Then comes the weekend. Everyone knows how busy Mondays are, so it's Tuesday or Wednesday before you can get to the contacts. By then you've forgotten a lot of the specifics. The enthusiasm is gone.

The faster you can follow up with them the better.

Suppose you know that it normally takes five or six calls over a six- to-eight-week period to get an attorney to commit to give you a case. You put together a follow-up grid. You plug all of the best prospects into that grid at the show.

I know someone who after she sets up her booth takes a selfie with her cell phone. When people come by her booth, guess what she does? She sends that video in an email to them. They are walking down the aisle, and all of a sudden they get this pop-up. They look at it and it's, "Hi this is Susan. I want to thank you for stopping by our booth. I really enjoyed visiting with you and look forward to getting back with you." It's little things like that and then staying with the follow up that make the difference. Unfortunately, 80% of trade show leads go un-worked.

Being memorable is key. Invest your exhibiting dollars wisely in terms of picking the show, the premiums, and the graphics. Ask questions that will help you qualify that prospect. Quickly address that person's need and then go into more depth in follow-up conversations.

In Conclusion

Overall, I highly recommend that you pursue trade shows and conventions. While they involve a lot of work and financial investment, they are the surest way to provide face-to-face conversations with attorneys. When you use the above guidelines, you can see a significant increase in your client base.

There is so much more I can share about exhibiting. Order a copy of my book, *Legal Nurse Consultant Marketing*, for more detailed tips about how to succeed at exhibiting. Order it at **http://lnc.tips/Creating series**.

Key Points

- Focus on two or three key areas of expertise when you exhibit.

- Be engaging when you are at your booth.

- Ask well prepared questions to qualify prospects. Encourage people who are not qualified to quickly leave your booth.

- Limit conversations about specific cases to a time when you are better able to concentrate and focus your attention.

- Aim to get quality leads rather than a quantity of leads who may not be qualified.

- Be prepared to handle the objection, "I already have an LNC."

- Trade shows are not necessarily about selling but rather bout building relationships.

- It is never too soon to follow up.

- Follow booth etiquette guidelines in order to get the most from your exhibiting experience.

CHAPTER 20

Top 13 Tips for Exhibiting at Attorney Conferences

You've spent a lot of money and time getting ready to exhibit at a conference. Don't waste your money by decreasing your effectiveness.

1. Don't play cards at your booth. Your goal is to be ready to talk to visitors.

2. Don't talk on your cell phone when you are at your booth. Attorneys will not approach you if you are on the phone. Be alert, look ready to start a conversation, and scan the room looking for people you may know. Be prepared to focus on your visitor, not on your phone.

3. Don't leave your laptop or purse or anything valuable in plain sight and unattended. This is an invitation for theft.

4. Don't have animated conversations with people at nearby booths or within your booth while attorneys are circulating in the exhibit area. This will discourage attorneys from approaching you.

5. Don't walk over to talk to another exhibitor while an attorney is at his booth. The interruption will annoy both the attorney and exhibitor. When the attor-

ney moves away from the booth, that is your signal to approach.

6. Don't give away food that is not wrapped. Donut holes, for example, are covered with sticky sugar. If a visitor puts his hands into a bowl, he encounters everyone else's germs.

7. Try to time your breaks or trips to the bathroom for times when the exhibit area is empty. Hide anything that is valuable while you leave the booth unattended.

8. Don't eat or drink in your booth. It is hard to have intelligent conversations with food in your mouth. Move to another area of the space to eat.

9. If you are involved in a 2-day exhibit and have collected business cards, don't leave them overnight in the collection bowl. Take them with you at the end of the day. You worked hard to get those cards. You don't want them to disappear.

10. Don't let your name badge flip over so that it's unreadable. Glance down and check it periodically.

11. Don't misrepresent yourself or your experience. I know of an LNC who told attorneys when she exhibited that she had clients in all 50 states and that she had the biggest LNC firm on the East Coast. Neither was true.

12. Don't fail to rapidly follow up with attorneys who have a case. The longer you wait, the less likely the attorney is to remember your conversation.

13. Have comfortable shoes to wear in the booth.

Let's Chat

Has this book reinforced or expanded your knowledge about marketing? Have you learned new concepts and techniques for obtaining more work? I hope so.

It is really easy to slide into inertia. But legal nurse consultants, like any small business owner, need to continually innovate and try new techniques. One of the reasons my LNC business was so successful was that I learned from my coach. I applied the marketing techniques he taught and they worked.

Where does the support and knowledge come from that you need to grow? No business owner is successful alone. Coaches and colleague provide new perspectives, support and accountability.

Are you ready to take action? Are you ready to take risks and try new things? Are you ready to feel support and have a community of colleagues to turn to?

I work with LNCs who are committed to their businesses, who want to grow, and know they need support. The people who get the most from having me as an LNC business coach want to get more clients, make more money and avoid expensive mistakes.

Complete this brief application to see if we are a good fit. http://lnc.tips/consult.

Thank you for buying this book. Now take action!

Consider Writing a Review

Thank you for buying this book. When you enjoy a book, it is a natural desire to tell others about it. Amazon.com provides a way to share your thoughts and I invite you to write a book review. It is easy. Here are tips:

1. After going to the link below on Amazon.com, the first thing you are asked to do is to assign a number of stars to the book you think matches your opinion of the book.

2. Create a title for the review. This can be a simple phrase, like "Awesome guide." If you are not sure what to say, look at the titles of other book reviews.

3. It is easiest to write the book in a word processor and then paste it into Amazon.com. Your word processor will pick up typos before your review goes public.

4. Write the review as if you were talking to another person — you are — a person who comes to Amazon.com and is considering buying this book.

5. Include a description of what you found most helpful. Was it an idea, chapter, tip? Share that with the readers.

6. Next you may want to write who you think would most benefit from this book. Is it for beginners? Or is it more appropriate for someone with experience with this topic?

7. What if you have something negative to say about the book? You may always reach me at patiyer@ legalnursebusiness.com to suggest changes in the book.

8. If you include negative feedback in the review, keep a positive perspective rather than attack the author.

Here are some sample phrases:

- While overall the book was good, I would change it by. . .
- I don't think this book is right for. . .
- I would improve this book by. . .

Before you hit save, read everything over one more time.

Authors and readers appreciate book reviews and they get easier to write with time. Go to this link on Amazon.com to write your review. If for any reason it does not work, search for the book title + Iyer and it will show.

Link:

Thank you,

Pat Iyer

Made in the USA
Middletown, DE
19 August 2019